The Heart of Motherhood

Also by Donna-Marie Cooper O'Boyle

Catholic Prayer Book for Mothers

The Heart of Motherhood

Finding Holiness
in the
Catholic Home

DONNA-MARIE COOPER O'BOYLE

A Crossroad Book
The Crossroad Publishing Company
New York

The Crossroad Publishing Company
831 Chestnut Ridge Road
Chestnut Ridge, NY 10977

Printed in the United States of America

The text of this book is set in 12/16 Cochin.
The display faces are Amadeus, Deepdene, Liberty, and Nuptial.

Printed in the United States of America

O'Boyle, Donna-Marie Cooper.
    The Heart of motherhood : finding holiness in the Catholic home / Donna-Marie Cooper O'Boyle.
        p. cm.
    ISBN-13: 978-0-8245-2403-6 (alk. paper)
    ISBN-10: 0-8245-2403-9 (alk. paper)
    1. Mothers – Religious life. 2. Motherhood – Religious aspects – Catholic Church. 3. Family – Religious aspects – Catholic Church.   I. Title.
BX2353.O26 2006
248.8′431088282 – dc22

                                                    2006021805

    2   3   4   5   6   7   8   9   10   12   11   10   09

With all my love and affection
to the most precious treasures of my life, my children:
Justin, Chaldea, Jessica, Joseph, and Mary-Catherine.
Each one of you in your own beautiful and unique way
has been a continuous profound source of love and
direction in my vocation of motherhood.
I immensely appreciate and cherish
my journey with all of you!

Words from
Blessed Teresa of Calcutta

"Your books on mothers and expectant mothers are much needed. Yes, you may use some of the things I said on motherhood and family. I pray that God may bless your endeavors."

After reading the author's manuscripts, Blessed Mother Teresa wrote: "My gratitude is my prayer for you that you may grow in the love of God through your beautiful thoughts of prayer you write and thus share with others."

She instructed, "God has given you many gifts — make sure you use them for the glory of God and the good of the people. You will then make your life something beautiful for God. You have been created to be holy. I assure you of my prayers and hope you pray for me also. Keep the joy of loving Jesus ever burning in your heart and share this joy with others."

On another occasion, she said, "I am very glad that you are using the gift God gave you to spread his love and mercy to all."

About this book, Mother Teresa said, "I pray that it does much good."

Fidelity to growing into a soul of prayer is the beginning of great holiness. If we remember "what we do to Jesus — that we do to each other," we would be real contemplatives in the heart of the world. Let us learn to pray and work as Jesus did for thirty years in Nazareth. The life and work, the prayer and sacrifice at Nazareth are so much like what our life should be. That peace, joy, and unity that joined the Holy Family together in prayer and work is such a wonderful living example to us. They grew in holiness together. Let us learn from Mary to pray and ask her to pray that your home will be another Nazareth.

Apostolic Blessing from Pope John Paul II

Shortly after the beatification of Blessed Teresa of Calcutta, Pope John Paul II imparted his apostolic blessing on Donna-Marie Cooper O'Boyle, her family, and her work *"as a pledge of joy and peace in our Lord Jesus Christ,"* and he promised his prayers and good wishes for Donna-Marie Cooper O'Boyle's work and writings on Mother Teresa of Calcutta (October 30, 2003).

Contents

Foreword

Donna's *The Heart of Motherhood* is a fine meditative work of domestic wisdom, worthy to be addressed to and studied by all modern mothers. With divorce, premarital sex, and millions of babies being born out of wedlock, it is apparent that the sacredness of marriage, home, and family are under severe attack. Donna's hope is that the readers of her book will meditate on the sacredness of marriage, home, and motherhood.

Her emphasis on personal and family prayer is needed today to keep the family together and make the home a holy place. Her frequent references to the domestic virtues of the holy home at Nazareth, with Mother Mary's loving, kind, gentle, and patient presence, is worth frequent meditation by modern-day mothers. This is followed, hopefully, by imitation in their homes.

Donna's book shows the role of motherhood to be, often, a back-breaking task. Mothers, like Martha, are "busy about many things," yet like Mary, sit at Jesus' feet in adoration and prayer as often as possible.

This book is theologically correct and offers sound, practical advice for domestic happiness for families living in these troubled times. May the Holy Family of Jesus, Mary, and Joseph bless Donna's efforts. May the sanctification of your individual homes earn the much-needed plea: "God bless America!"

Rev. William C. Smith
Norwalk, Connecticut

Introduction

I prayed for this child, and the Lord granted my request. Now I, in turn, give him to the Lord; as long as he lives, he shall be dedicated to the Lord. — 1 Samuel 1:27–28

How can we profess faith in God's Word, and then refuse to let it inspire our thinking, our activity, our decisions, and our responsibilities toward one another? Faith is always demanding because faith leads us beyond ourselves. Faith imparts a vision of life's purpose and stimulates us to action. — Pope John Paul II

A mother's efforts in the home are unlikely to make the headlines or earn any kind of prestigious award. But we should never forget that the love, devotion, and care a mother puts into her seemingly ordinary tasks makes them in fact, extraordinary. God put her in the heart of the home, where she helps to ensure her family's salvation in her role as a source of love, guidance, solace, and comfort for all around her.

I think we can all agree that mothers in our day could use some encouragement and recognition. Unfortunately, our world makes it hard to be proud of the title "mother." We do know, though, that motherhood is a remarkable and sublime role. It is a shame that mothers feel pressure from society, which dictates that one's worth is measured only by one's paycheck. Pope John Paul II told us in *Evangelium Vitae,* "In living out their mission, these heroic women do not always find support in the world around them. On the contrary, the cultural models frequently promoted and broadcast by the media do not encourage motherhood. In the name of progress and modernity the values of fidelity, chastity, sacrifice to which a host of Christian wives and mothers have borne and continue to bear outstanding witness, are presented as obsolete." We see the need to pray that our society will realize the intrinsic value of motherhood.

"The family should be your place of encounter with God," we were also told by Pope John Paul II. As mothers, we need to realize that this is indeed true. We meet God each day in the smiles and in the tears of our children. He is there in our laundry rooms as we work hard, keeping things clean and in order for our families. He is present during our intimate dinner conversations, during our disagreements, and also in the quiet of the home. He is deep down in the hearts of our families.

We are grateful to our own mothers for our very existence. It would be wonderful if more mothers could be at home, content with caring for their children. My hope is that I can help more mothers realize and embrace the sublimity of their missions as mothers, responsible for the souls entrusted to their care.

Our Lord certainly favors mothers. He enters into a partnership with them to create human life — an incredible miracle and mystery! Mothers possess the power to be an incredible example to others around them. They make a significant impact on the world, merely by lovingly performing many tasks of selfless service within their families.

A dedicated mother also recognizes the quintessential power in a mother's prayer where innumerable graces are granted. She knows, too, that prayer is essential for her family's health and survival. How can a mother, inundated with the care of her family, actually find time for prayer? How can she focus on prayer when she must focus on the task at hand with her children?

The key to a mother's inner peace is to find that marvelous balance between a prayerful life and her family life. A faithful mother soon learns that, in order to survive, her life should really *become* a prayer.

Allow the lessons of love in this book to assist you in keeping your heart lifted always toward Heaven even as your hands and mind are occupied with your many and varied tasks in your vocation of motherhood. May God bless you and your beautiful family in abundance!

It is a disservice not only to children but also to women and society itself when a woman is made to feel guilty for wanting to remain in the home and nurture and care for her children. It is also necessary to counter the misconception that the role of motherhood is oppressive to women and that a commitment to her family, particularly to her children, prevents a woman from reaching personal fulfillment and from having an influence in society. No response to woman's issues can ignore a woman's role in the family or take lightly the fact that every new life is entrusted to the protection and care of the woman carrying it in the womb. — Pope John Paul II

ONE

Our World Needs Saints

We must deepen our life of love, prayer, and sacrifice, for compassion, love, and understanding have to grow from within and from our union with Christ.

— Blessed Teresa of Calcutta

We live in an era that is desperately in need of saints to evangelize our world. Pope John Paul II told us, "We must supplicate the Lord to increase the Church's spirit of holiness and to send us new saints to evangelize today's world; more than reformers [the Church] has a need for saints, because saints are the authentic and most fruitful reformers."

Pope Benedict XVI reiterated the importance of the laity's role in evangelization when he said they "represent a source of great wealth for the Church." He added that "One of the chief aims of the activity of the laity is the moral renewal of society, which cannot be superficial, partial, and instantaneous."

Reflecting on Jesus' words in Scripture when he said, "The Kingdom of Heaven is like the yeast a woman took and mixed in with three measures of flour till it was leavened all through," we realize that just as a little yeast can leaven a batch of bread dough to feed the whole family, so can the holiness of a few people have a great influence in the Church and the world.

Consider Blessed Teresa of Calcutta, whom I had the wonderful privilege of knowing. She was less than five feet tall, hunched over in humility and from her constant stooping to serve the poorest of the poor, who oftentimes lay on mats on the floor.

Having been called she gave her life totally to the Lord when she became a nun. Then she received another distinct call from God, an inner conviction that she was to take care of his poor, "the poorest of the poor," as she called them. So, she just went out and did it. There was never a hint of hesitation in her heart or in her step. Though she didn't know how she could accomplish this massive task, as a woman small in stature, she wouldn't allow the questions plaguing her mind to stop her from following God's holy will.

✍ *Making a Difference, One by One*

After seeking and receiving permission from her superiors and then from the Church's hierarchy to follow the Lord's call, Blessed Teresa proceeded. She left the comfort of her convent to go out to the filthy streets of Calcutta in search for Jesus in the "distressing disguise of the poorest of the poor," as she described it.

She did not set out to change the whole world single-handedly. She knew she could not feed all the world's hungry or clothe all the naked, give solace to all who mourned, or comfort to all those who suffered. She knew she couldn't possibly befriend all of the lonely. These thoughts did not overwhelm her or cause her to pause to doubt herself. She remained steadfast in her faith and truly dependent on God's divine providence.

Blessed Teresa was determined to help each person she came into contact with, individually, one by one. She saw our Lord Jesus' face in the faces of all who suffered. She wanted to ease the pain of and bring peace to the distraught and the dying, even if only for a few moments before they left this earthly life. This she did in a truly selfless and extraordinary way, putting her own physical needs aside, working long hours on her feet to minister to everyone she came in contact with.

Blessed Teresa felt called by God to open houses for the dying all over the world, an undertaking she began in Calcutta. The poor, who would have died unnoticed in the streets of Calcutta, were instead picked up from the streets by Blessed Teresa and her sisters and brought to the houses of dying where they were cared for with deep respect and love. Many of these people who died in those houses had never felt a loving human touch prior to entering the houses. Each person who died in one of her houses of dying is said to have come to know Jesus and become totally peaceful before breathing their last breath. Just as Blessed Teresa and her sisters saw Jesus in those they cared for, the sick and dying were also able to see Jesus in the sisters, which was exactly what they needed before they left this life on earth. The selfless and prayerful love in action allowed these beautiful and transforming occurrences to take place.

Blessed Teresa began her work on her own. To her vows of poverty, chastity, and obedience she added a fourth vow of "wholehearted free service to the poorest of the poor." Her strong conviction about the necessity of her work was based on a selfless life of deep and constant prayer wanting to serve Jesus as he had never yet been served, as well as her total surrender to her lover's will.

One by one, the other sisters came to join her and the Missionaries of Charity order was formed. Over the years, the number of sisters has multiplied to the thousands. The Missionaries of Charity order now has convents, shelters, soup kitchens, orphanages, and homes for the dying all over the world. Before she died, Blessed Teresa even managed to open houses in areas difficult to get into, including Russia and Cuba.

Blessed Teresa of Calcutta is one example of what can happen when a prayerful, humble woman simply follows God's holy will in her life. By God's grace, this prayerful woman unquestionably deeply and profoundly affected the entire world.

Her vision and her legacy will live on forever in the hearts and minds of people from every walk of life. Even though she has left this earthly life, her work continues through her sisters, priests, brothers, co-workers, lay Missionaries of Charity, the faithful, and all whom she has influenced by her life of extreme love.

She gave all credit to God always. She said she was "just a little stubby pencil in our Lord's hand," referring to the fact that God used her as he wanted, to spread his word and live his love. However, you can't do God's work quietly to the extent that Mother Teresa was doing it, affecting such a large population, without attracting publicity.

Mother Teresa accepted all the awards given to her in the name of the poor. She refused to get political and went straight to the task at hand. Because this one woman listened to God's promptings in her heart and soul, desired to do his will, and responded with a wholehearted "yes" in love and service, she ministered to millions and she inspired millions of others to follow in her footsteps.

✍ *Mother Teresa and All Mothers*

It may seem strange to begin a book concerning the call to holiness for mothers with a description of a nun, who, although she was a Mother to her order, the Missionaries of Charity, never biologically mothered a child. I have used Blessed Teresa to point out that just as her own response to God's call to holiness profoundly influenced many others, so too, does a dedicated mother's response, when she opens her heart to our Lord's will and to her vocation as a mother.

Blessed Teresa of Calcutta was a simple, humble, and prayerful woman. Prior to answering God's call to start the Missionaries of Charity to serve the poor, she was often overlooked during her life at the convent in Loreto and not really given a second thought. To her fellow nuns, she seemed to be a very ordinary woman, somewhat frail, no one significant.

What made her extraordinary was her wholehearted willingness to follow our Lord's will in her life when she received his call. And because of God's miraculous ways, this one woman's "yes" has affected countless souls.

In the same way, prayerful mothers can be an extraordinary inspiration to others. Just as Mother Teresa saw Jesus in all whom she met, a mother sees the Creator in her children. A mother's dedication to and love for her family not only influences her family, but is also carried out into the world. It all starts with a desiring heart, which we all can possess. When the gift of life is bestowed upon a mother, she also receives the graces to carry out her calling as a mother. With prayer and God's grace she will naturally aspire to fulfill her duties well, making a positive impact on the world.

May we heed Pope John Paul II's request and "supplicate our Lord," begging for more saints in our present age to help effect major changes in our world. I have heard Blessed Teresa state numerous times, "Holiness is not a luxury for a few, but a duty for everyone."

We cannot sit around waiting for someone else to do our Lord's work. We need to realize that we are all called to be saints in all our walks of life, and we must open our hearts to hear our Lord calling to us. There's work to be done. We have our work cut out for us.

We have seen what miraculous things took place when one person listened to our Lord and decided to follow his holy will in her life. Just imagine what could happen if we all listened and truly followed him, one foot in front of the other in all of our own paths through life. Mothers can, indeed, make a tremendous difference in human hearts and in the world as we search out Jesus "in the distressing disguise of our families."

PRAYER TO
BLESSED TERESA OF CALCUTTA
AND THE BLESSED MOTHER

Blessed Teresa of Calcutta, Jesus called you to be the light of his love to the world. By God's grace, you were drawn to the thirsting love of Jesus on the Cross and allowed it to become a living flame burning within you. Please obtain from the Heart of Jesus (here make your request). Teach me to allow Jesus to penetrate and possess my whole being so completely that my life, too, may radiate his light and love to others. Immaculate Heart of Mary, Cause of our Joy, pray for me. Blessed Teresa of Calcutta, please pray for me. Amen.

LIVE AND SHINE
THROUGH ME, LORD

Dear Jesus, please help me to become united to you as I prayerfully journey through my life. Please increase the desire in my heart to bring others closer to you. As I mother my children, helping them to light their lamps, please radiate my own lamp so brilliantly that others who come to know me will see your heart burning within me, lighting the way for others. Amen.

TWO

The Ordinary Yet Quite Extraordinary Vocation

The child is the beauty of God present in the world, the greatest gift to the family.

— Blessed Teresa of Calcutta

We cannot all be Blessed Mother Teresas. We cannot and *should not* (those of us with small children to raise) drop everything and run off to Calcutta or some other poverty-stricken area to try and change the world. We can, though, in our own families, be instrumental in creating major changes. For a mother, this is far more meritorious than trying to convert the entire world, believe it or not!

This is not to say that no mothers will ever travel to other areas of the globe to bring healing and solace to others, if they are so called. But everything must be in its proper time frame, first things first. We begin in our families. Love begins at home.

A faithful mother, by her loving, diligent example will turn heads and hearts. She will edify others through her strong faith in God and her unfailing dedication to her family. Her selflessness and self-giving will be apparent to the individuals around her whom she is influencing and inspiring by her life of love. She may never be aware of this, but our Lord will know.

Although a good part of our society does not give a second thought to a mother's role, her love and dedication can have a profound effect on other lives. How can this be?

Households can seem very chaotic and are stressful at times. Hardly the appearance of holiness, it would seem. Throughout these hectic and sometimes crazy times, a mother often needs to practice the heroic virtues to get through life's everyday trials.

By heroic, I mean self-sacrificing. By her practicing such virtues, she and her family will shine even during stressful or troubled times, all the while searching for the joy in life.

There are many saintly mothers in our midst today, sometimes humbly hidden within their families. They do what comes naturally to them: they love their children; they make their home a strong, warm, secure haven for their families. They set a caring example.

A mother's day is filled to capacity with many ordinary tasks, not unimportant, but rather works of love that may be overlooked or unnoticed. Changing diapers, doing laundry, schedule keeping, house cleaning, planning and cooking nutritious meals, and helping with homework are just some of the ordinary tasks in a mom's repertoire. Her own family may take these loving acts for granted. Although these tasks may seem mundane or even monotonous, they are the nitty-gritty details that keep the family going and together.

Mothers perform their never-ending labors of love throughout each day, precisely because of the love they possess for their children. A mother's deep inner faith affirms that a day's sacrifices and seemingly ordinary tasks please our Lord because they are done with extraordinary love.

✒ *Do All That We Do with Love*

St. Thérèse of Lisieux, a beloved saint known for her simplicity and total abandonment to God, said, "Remember that nothing is small in the eyes of God. Do all that you do with love." We mothers should remember these beautiful words when we are feeding our infant in the wee hours of the morning, changing diapers, wiping our children's tears and giving them a hug, bringing peace to bickering siblings, playing a game, helping with homework, rescuing our kids from a bad situation, filling out college forms, giving them our love and attention, praise and encouragement, or putting dinner on the table. All that we do, we do with love, and our Lord is truly pleased. Nothing is small in his eyes. Amazing!

Blessed Teresa of Calcutta agreed with St. Thèrèse when she preached, "Small things done with great love bring peace and love." When we look back at the most significant and memorable experiences we had in our youth, we all seem to recall that the extremely meaningful moments in our lives were rooted in very simple acts of love. Yet, when we stop to think about love, it is never really simple; rather, it is miraculous. The beautiful words expressed in the First Letter of John are brought to mind: "God is love, and he who abides in love abides in God, and God abides in him" (1 John 4:16).

Mothers encounter God within their families every day in the sublime mission our Lord has entrusted to them in the heart of the home. He has put the mother in the midst of her family where she, by her word, love, life, and example, raises up soldiers for Jesus Christ.

Both parents have an equal responsibility in bringing souls into the world and then raising them and educating them for eternal salvation. But mothers, because of the central nature of their role with their children, have this responsibility in a much more immediate, direct, and hands-on way.

A mother's day is chock-full of many "small things done with great love." Although some of a mother's tasks may seem small and insignificant, on a larger scale her children depend on her for their very lives, from the moment of their conception, actually even from before conception.

Prayer is desperately needed today for mothers so that they will themselves feel compelled to pray for all of the necessary graces to faithfully fulfill their duties as mothers. Prayer is needed for the children who spend their days with nonfamily members at day-care centers and with babysitters, thus missing the benefit of being raised solely by their parents.

Many mothers who are not at peace with the sometimes humdrum tasks in the home may seek freedom outside the home, engaging in activities and employment that takes them away from their children.

Sometimes financial reasons are stated for the need for a mother to be employed. I am not condemning or judging any mother who sincerely needs to earn wages to help support her family.

I do hope, however, that mothers can arrange their work schedule to be available to their children as much as possible. In addition to this, mothers should be certain that their children will be well cared for, preferably by relatives who have a genuine love and concern for their children, rather than by strangers whose influence is different than ours. Children truly need a mother's love and presence. This presence is crucial, so do try to plan your life accordingly.

∽ *The Power in a Mother's Love*

The Missionaries of Charity sisters in Calcutta and Blessed Teresa welcomed a little starving girl they had found in the streets home to their convent one time. The little girl was very thin and dirty. She began to thrive on the love and good food she was fed at the convent. After a few days, though, she went missing. Blessed Teresa had the sisters search for her. They found her under a tree with her mother and siblings. The little girl had left the safety and warmth of the convent, the good food and clean clothes, to return to her mother under the tree. Home is in your mother's eyes, they say. Under the tree, the family found their home in their mother's sheltering love. A mother's love is powerful!

Let us remember that *love* is not merely a feeling or emotion. Love is also a decision. Mothers need to decide to make the very best choices possible for their children at *all* times. Staying home and caring for our children, when it is possible, is not a luxury; it is a decision. At times, this decision may be an enormous sacrifice to a woman who takes pride in her successes and accomplishments outside the home.

Society, in particular, and families must respect the mother's domestic role at home. Pope John Paul II was very clear about this: "The mentality which honors women more for their work outside the home than for their work within the family must be overcome. This requires that men should esteem and love women with total respect for their personal dignity, and that society should create and develop conditions favoring work in the home."

We can start by helping to bring back the dignity and respect motherhood deserves, by our example of our holy mothering, which will make an impact on society.

There are certainly many broken, unhappy families. It often seems that all good values and morals have been forgotten. It is no wonder that motherhood has been denigrated. Since the family is truly the basic unit of society, when they are in turmoil, families can cause the whole world to appear chaotic.

⌒ *Family Is Society's Primary Vital Cell*

God has given the family an awesome role and responsibility. "The mission of being the primary vital cell of society has been given to the family by God Himself" (Decree on the Apostolate of the Laity, Vatican Council II, no. 11).

There is a great need for model families in our world today. By remaining simple and focused, dedicated to following God's will through the vocation of motherhood, mothers can be a radiant example to others. These mothers can encourage other mothers who are struggling without a prayer life and also those who feel pressured by society to work outside the home.

A genuine assessment is necessary to determine a household's real needs, without heeding to what the materialistic world dictates. Simplicity is a very good thing. Additionally, less material clutter can help tremendously to focus the heart. Expenses often can be cut down considerably.

Pope John Paul II told us, "May mothers, young women, and girls not listen to those who tell them that working a secular job, succeeding in a secular profession, is more important than the vocation of giving life and caring for this life as mother."

We need to pray for the mothers who struggle along without any help, trying their best to raise and protect their children from the world's evil influences. They need our help and support. They may be single mothers, widowed mothers, or mothers whose husbands don't take an interest in their children's welfare. We all need encouragement and prayer.

∽ Love Can Be Tiring

St. Vincent de Paul said, "Let us love God, but with the strength of our arms, in the sweat of our brow." Yes, loving God as a mother does require our arms to get weary as we carry around a fussy baby and as we carry out our tasks in the home. Our consolation is in knowing that God sees each bead of sweat on our brow as we strive to keep up with the never-ending chores of our household. If we are able to spare time and effort outside our families when we are sure our family's needs are fulfilled, we can reach out to help others in need in our communities.

Mothers' prayer groups can be established by mothers wanting to help fellow mothers, with the main purpose being the sanctification of the family members. The group's main apostolate or ministries could be programs started by the group to help needy families, expectant mothers, or single mothers in the community.

This may require some serious soul-searching. Although our hearts are huge and we want to help, we must first begin in our own homes. Blessed Teresa preached over and over again, "Love begins at home." There is where we begin our salvation and our family's salvation. It is truly in all of our loving acts each day.

When we are tired, we can also draw consolation from St. Dominic Savio, who said, "Nothing seems tiresome or painful when you are working for a Master who pays well; who rewards even a cup of cold water given for love of him." Mothers know all too well the numbers of glasses of water they bring to their children, never given begrudgingly, though sometimes given while exhausted. A mother's true reward will be in Heaven, but she can count her many blessings here on earth as she looks into the eyes of her children.

A mother's vocation is one of service, and a very privileged one at that. Our Lord calls us to serve and tells us that he will welcome us into the Kingdom of Heaven because we have served him in others. We can reflect on the Bible passage Matthew 25:34–46 (which was one of Blessed Teresa's favorite Scripture passages and which, along with deep prayer, continued to drive Blessed Teresa to serve Jesus in others): "Come, you who are blessed by my Father. Inherit the kingdom prepared for you from the foundation of the world. For I was hungry and you gave me food, I was thirsty and you gave me drink, a stranger and you welcomed me, naked and you clothed me, ill and you cared for me, in prison and you visited me." We can be utterly consoled knowing that we are serving Jesus in our family when we have truly dedicated ourselves in Jesus' service.

We hope that through our example and love, by God's grace, we will lead many souls to Heaven. Our purpose here on earth is to draw others to God by our life and love. Let us hope and pray that we can truly be God's instruments, drawing others to him by our lives of love.

Vatican II's vision of the laity's role was a call to all of us to evangelize the world through the "witness of our own faith." Let us pray for many more holy families to be an example to our world today. Let us also pray for the restoration of the natural order, with the role of motherhood again exalted to its proper dignity.

✌ *Take Five*

Many times, mothers feel guilty for "sitting down on the job." I know I found myself avoiding a rest time. Since there is always a tremendous amount of work to accomplish in the home before a day is through, many mothers deny themselves a short break or rest for fear of not getting all of their chores completed.

Most of us are usually cleaning up and folding laundry into the evening hours. We fall into our beds at night exhausted. There is no escaping the fact that a mother's work in the home is never really done. We are on call twenty-four hours a day, seven days a week, tending to our family's needs, especially when they are ill or in need of extra comfort and understanding.

Sometimes, we can become so involved in household chores that it can feel impossible to break away. A short break, when possible, is a welcome and certainly well-deserved diversion. It is actually good for our family, too, as it will keep us rested and healthy.

"Relaxation of the mind from work consists in playful words or deeds. Therefore it becomes a wise and virtuous person to have recourse to such things. It is necessary at times to make use of them, in order to give rest, as it were, to the soul," St. Thomas Aquinas said in *Summa Theologica*. Slowing down a bit also presents opportunities to be more aware of all the everyday blessings and simple pleasures in family life that we may pass right by.

I remember one time in particular when my little daughter tugged on my pants leg insisting, "Mommy, put your face here!" to get my full attention as I busily folded my family's laundry. Although I was right beside her, I could have missed her need to have my undivided attention at that moment in my panic to catch up with chores. As we go about our days in the care of our families and our households, we know that our children are usually happy and content having us bustling about nearby while we cook or clean. But, there are also the times we have to drop what we are doing (even if we are up to our elbows in a project!) to be really present to them.

We also want to be joyful and radiate that joy to our family. We don't want to feel resentful for not being able to get away from our work or become grouchy, unhappy, or frustrated and take it out on our families. By allowing ourselves at least a few short breaks during the day, we can take a breath, relax, or pursue something that interests us. Even a stroll in the sunshine with our youngsters is refreshing and a welcome change and will also give rest to the soul as we delight in time well spent with our children.

ᴄᴧ *Our Work Is Priceless*

Pope John Paul II often spoke about the equal dignity of men and women. His succinct words clearly dispel the idea that the Catholic Church considers women to be inferior to and subservient to men. The Roman Catholic Church does not profess this, in the least. Again and again, Pope John Paul II and now Benedict XVI reiterated the fact that men and women have equal dignity. Men and women have differing roles, which is only natural. We have been truly blessed with leaders such as Pope John Paul II and Benedict XVI who have promoted the advancement of women culturally, socially, and politically while defending our gift of motherhood.

Pope John Paul II also spoke about a woman's family role, comparing it to all other professions when he profoundly said, "There is no doubt that the equal dignity and responsibility of men and women fully justifies women's access to public functions. On the other hand the true advancement of women requires that clear recognition be given to the value of their maternal and family role, by comparison with all other public roles and all other professions. Furthermore, these roles and professions should be harmoniously combined, if we wish the evolution of society and culture to be truly and fully human."

He added, "While it must be recognized that women have the same right as men to perform various public functions, society must be structured in such a way that wives and mothers are not in practice compelled to work outside the home, and that their families can live and prosper in a dignified way even when they themselves devote their full time to their own family.

"Furthermore, the mentality which honors women more for their work outside the home than for their work within the family must be overcome. This requires that men should truly esteem and love women with total respect for their personal dignity, and that society should create and develop conditions favoring work in the home."

We know that women of today live with a jungle of contemporary messages from our society that allegedly promote us women. We are hit from every angle, informed that we need to liberate ourselves and imitate men. This liberation consequently denies our honorable and sublime roles as mothers. It is truly a shame and a scary fact that women are sometimes blinded by the devil's tactics and become victims of the persistent mentality in today's culture. The devil will stop at nothing to destroy the family, the primary vital cell of society that was given by God himself!

We cannot become complacent. Christian mothers need to be a contradiction to the world. We have to work and pray tirelessly to counteract the damage done and be a light to others. We need to go against the flow to do the right thing — the holy thing.

The devil would like women of the world to believe that it is the Catholic Church that degrades women, when in fact it is his own divisive plan to destroy the family and seduce everyone to hell. Strong words, yes, but true.

We can hope and pray that the ideals that Pope John Paul II spoke of will be achieved in our world — that women will be recognized and honored for their selfless invaluable work in the home. We must all do our part to insist that "the work of women in the home be recognized and respected by all in its irreplaceable value."

A MOTHER'S PRAYER TO JESUS

Dear Lord Jesus, thank you for the incredible gifts of my children. During the busyness of my journey through motherhood, help me to remember to call upon you for strength, grace, and guidance so I may raise my children properly. Help me to find and embrace the sublimity in my vocation of motherhood so I may be a radiant example to my children and to others as well. Amen.

LORD, HELP ME SEE

Dear Lord, help me to see the extraordinary graces that abound in a role that is sometimes thought of as ordinary. Please reinforce the dedication in my heart to raise my children with extreme love — love that knows no limits, love that is priceless. Help me to remember that there is immeasurable power in a mother's love and a mother's prayer for her children. Thank you, dear Lord, for this awesome gift! Amen.

THREE

Mary, Our Sublime Model

Take shelter under our Lady's mantle, and do not fear. She will give you all you need. She is very rich, and besides is very generous with her children. She loves giving.
— Blessed Raphaela Maria

Modern-day mothers surely need a lot of encouragement. It would be very helpful if priests and religious were to acknowledge the great importance of a mother's role in our society and do all that they can to encourage and commend mothers. There are not a lot of sources for mothers for pats on the back.

Mothers are up against incredible adversity. They have the enormous task of raising their children amidst the horrible, sometimes frightening temptations and seductions in our world, which come from the prince of darkness, whose task is to snatch children from their families. These are scary thoughts, thoughts we would rather avoid.

Attacks on the family come at us mercilessly from every side. Television broadcasts often attack family values. The Internet can be a gate for filth and evil to enter your home without your ever knowing it. A mother must be very aware and proactive in monitoring the influences on her children.

Mothers should be aware of what our children are taught at school. We should also take a close look at the company our children keep and steer them clear of bad company and bad influences. This is easier when children are young, of course, and more difficult when they are older and have more freedom.

The stimulus a child comes in contact with helps to mold his or her character. Even with a strong foundation of prayer, a stellar upbringing, and parental teaching and guidance, it is sometimes difficult for our children to make appropriate choices when they are bombarded by temptation to do otherwise. A mother has to filter all that comes to her children. It's not an easy job, especially when we are tired and inclined to let our guard down.

As cliché as it sounds, we need to keep the lines of communication open with our children. At every age and every stage of development that our children travel through, we should take the time to truly listen to them. This is half the battle, right here. Let's try not to be quick to interject our own thoughts and opinions during our conversations with them, as tempting as it is. We want to know what they are thinking and feeling. They are not going to open up to us when they feel us breathing down their necks ready to pounce. Sometimes this trust and comfort level is best achieved when out on a walk, tossing a ball around, or performing an activity, rather than sitting face to face, when our children might feel self-conscious or less inclined to reveal their true thoughts and feelings.

Truly, we need to try to hear what our children have to say, and then we can learn how much more direction they need from us. Good communication doesn't happen overnight. Hopefully we started developing this art form when they were young.

Remember that we are the parents, not the best friends, and we love our children dearly. Since we are genuinely our children's first teacher as well as their most important teacher, we must hold tight to our values and teachings of the truth about God. Don't let the truth get watered down by the ever-present "I'm okay, you're okay" attitude in our midst, that anything is okay as long as it feels good. Above and beyond any other teacher, we have the immediate duty to instill the proper teachings into our children.

✍ *Mary's Feet Continue to Crush the Serpent*

Mothers should call upon our Blessed Mother, whose holy feet crushed the head of the serpent. God gave tremendous, limitless power to Mother Mary, who once walked this earth, mothering our Lord Jesus.

D. Roberto, Hermit of Monte Corona, said, "Yes, she crushed and continues to crush his head; howsoever much he may foam, and rage, and storm, he must remain oppressed, bound, and crushed under the most strong foot of Mary." St. Louis de Montfort said, "The humble Mary will always have the victory over that proud spirit [Satan], and so great a victory that she will go so far as to crush his head, where his pride dwells. She will always discover the malice of the serpent. She will always lay bare his infernal plots and dissipate his diabolical counsels, and even to the end of time will guard her faithful servants from his cruel claw."

St. Bernardine of Siena said, "Crushed and trodden under the feet of Mary, he suffers a miserable slavery." Thomas à Kempis said, "At the name of Mary, the devils are prostrated as by a thunderbolt from Heaven."

Mothers can and should pray to Mary and strive to imitate her virtues. Mothers and children will greatly benefit from praying the rosary together. The prayer of the rosary will never be outdated; it is not only a lovely remembrance of Jesus' and the Blessed Mother's life, but is a powerful weapon against evil. Even a single Hail Mary is a powerful prayer, invoking the Blessed Mother's help and protection. We can begin praying the rosary with our children when they are still babies.

As our children grow older, decades of the rosary can be recited together as a family. However, prayer should never be forced upon children. Prayer is a conversation with the Divine and should be treated as such. When teaching our children to pray, we should try not to inadvertently turn our children away from prayer by being unrealistic in what we expect from them or by becoming overly regimented with them.

Prayer is a way of life, and it will become natural to children when it is taught to them when they are young. Our children will learn to turn to prayer when in need and also, hopefully, in thanksgiving and later on, just because they love the Lord. Setting a prayerful example for them is much more articulate than harping at them to pray could ever be. Encourage, yes; harp, no!

A holy life within the family at home imitates Mary's life with her husband, Joseph, and her son, Jesus, in Nazareth. We can be certain that Mary went about her duties lovingly and meticulously, knowing that in serving her family, she was fulfilling her first responsibility in our Lord's eyes.

We, too, often remain at home, apart from the community at large, when we have a newborn baby or several small children to care for. We can meditate on Mary's quiet hidden life in Nazareth, content with our season of quiet. In our "hidden life," if we look carefully, we can find many occasions for prayer even though we are busy with our family. The Blessed Mother can teach us to pray and help us to find the opportunities for prayer.

Because of the changing seasons in a mother's life, before too long we find ourselves out and about in the hustle and bustle of the world. There, too, we find our place. Our children's activities and our services to a neighbor or the less fortunate will bring us into contact with others. This may not only be a welcome change from the confinement of our household, but may refresh others as well as ourselves.

We should remember that Mary was faced with many trials as she mothered our Lord Jesus. The Decree on the Apostolate of the Laity states that lay people are encouraged to emulate Mary because she blends perfectly the spiritual and apostolic life. "Indeed, while leading a life common to us, one filled with family concerns and labors, Mary was always intimately united to Christ, furthering the work of the Savior." The document concludes that "all should devoutly venerate her and commend their life and apostolate to her maternal care."

Throughout our life's trials and tribulations, we can find solace knowing that we can look to Mary, our Immaculate Mother, for comfort and guidance. Our Blessed Mother certainly experienced incomparable sweet joys, mothering our Lord, but we should be mindful of the fact that she also experienced tremendous pain and suffering during her earthly life. She was human like us. Her heart was pierced through with a sword of sorrow. She partook in her son's grief and sufferings as he evangelized the world and was persecuted by many. Mary must have experienced intense agony as she helplessly watched her son go to his death. Mary was not a mere observer. She actually walked Calvary with her son, experiencing each and every pain and torment with him, as only a mother can, and then finally witnessed his agonizing death on the Cross.

Mary held her son's lifeless, blood-streaked body against her breast after his death when he was placed in her arms after being brought down from the Cross. She embraced his body, tears undoubtedly streaming down her face, as she held her son, Jesus, close and prayed to her Father in Heaven.

As mothers, we can strive to imitate Mary's virtues and ask for her help in finding the balance in our spiritual and apostolic life. She will help us unite our souls to Jesus, so we may further his work in our homes and in society.

⌒ *Mary Longs to Be Your Mother*

> *Her conversation has no bitterness, nor her company any tediousness, but joy and gladness.* — Wisdom 8:16

Mary, our Blessed Mother, is the highest expression of the feminine genius seen by our Church, and we find in her a source of constant inspiration. In Luke 1:38 she calls herself the "handmaid of the Lord" and illustrates that "nothing is impossible for God" if we open our heart and conform our will to his plan.

Although Mary was the mother of Jesus, she was also human like us and needed to be steadfast in her faith and prayer, which required effort on her part. She attended to the needs of others in her role as the Blessed Mother, much as we mothers are called to do. Her "yes" to God's call to the vocation of the mother of Jesus and a life she would lead in service to others continues today, as she serves us with her intercessory prayer.

Pope Benedict XVI recalled the image of Mary as she appears in Dante's *Divine Comedy,* "humbler and higher than all other creatures, fixed aim and goal of the eternal plan," adding, "in contemplating the Virgin, how can we not reawaken in ourselves, her children, the aspiration to beauty, goodness and purity of heart?"

"Her celestial candor," Pope Benedict XVI said, "attracts us towards God, helping us to overcome the temptation to a mediocre life — one made up of compromises with evil — and orienting us decisively towards authentic goodness, which is a source of joy."

Call upon Mary often. Get to know her through your prayers to her. Pray the rosary even if you only have time for bits and pieces. Our Lord knows your heart, and so does his Blessed Mother. She longs to be your

Mother. She is the mediatrix of all graces and a sure means to get closer to Jesus. She calls us to goodness and purity of heart. She helps us to run from the temptation of mediocrity and compromises.

St. Bernardine said that God alone knows the beauty of Mary's soul, and we should know that she is a "paradise of delights." If we desire to be happy and blessed, not only in the other life but also in this "valley of misery and tears," there is no more certain and secure means than the "conversation, society, and love of so amiable a Lady."

We know how truly selfless our Blessed Mother was and is still now. One illustration of her selfless love was in her decision and journey to visit her cousin, Elizabeth. Even though Mary was pregnant with our Lord, she reached out to help someone else whom Mary felt must surely need a hand, since Elizabeth was also expecting a child, but was much older.

When reflecting on Mary's visit to help St. Elizabeth, Blessed Teresa of Calcutta said, "Our Lady, the most beautiful of all women, the greatest, the humblest, the most pure, the most holy, the moment she felt she was full of grace, full of Jesus, went in haste — and here she is a model for all women — by sharing immediately what she received. This is, so to say, like the breaking of the Eucharist; and we know what happened to St. John the Baptist; he leapt with joy at the presence of Christ."

By getting to know the Blessed Mother through prayer, we may begin to emulate her actions of sharing what she received from God, for she is a model for all women as Blessed Teresa pointed out. God truly fashioned a woman's heart to be nurturing and giving and a healing medicine of love to all around her, as Mary so clearly exemplifies.

Pope John Paul II, as we know, had a great love for the Blessed Mother. His motto, "Totus Tuus," or "I am totally yours," he told us meant to him "To Jesus through Mary." He also told us, "Love the simple, fruitful prayer of the rosary." Blessed Teresa of Calcutta had a very beautiful and intimate relationship with Blessed Mother Mary. Blessed Teresa prayed the rosary constantly and instructed her sisters to pray it, especially during arduous or dangerous times. Her convents are mostly located in areas that have a reputation for exposure to danger. She purposely chose these locations to be near those most in need. The prayer of the rosary is an excellent means to grow in holiness; additionally, it helps to protect us. Blessed Teresa's sisters pray the rosary when walking through the streets going to those they minister to, which usually means traveling through precarious or dangerous situations. They have always been protected.

Blessed Teresa encouraged many of the people she met to call upon the Blessed Mother when they felt scared or in need of help or consolation. In addition to other prayers, she said we should pray these simple words: "Mary, Mother of Jesus, be a mother to me now." This is a simple, succinct, but powerful prayer that can be said anytime. Keep it in your heart and say it often.

When I was on complete bed rest because of a very complicated high-risk pregnancy with my fifth child, Mary-Catherine, Blessed Mother Teresa told me to ask Mother Mary to "be a mother to me now." She told me not to be afraid and to call upon Mary often. She told me to wear a Miraculous Medal that she had given me, and she said the Blessed Mother had helped many who had worn her medal and asked for her help. She reassured me that the Blessed Mother would also help me. And without a doubt, she did!

We can strive to emulate Mary, our Blessed Mother, and to find it in our hearts to also say, "Let it be done to me according to thy word."

CONSECRATION OF A CHILD
TO THE BLESSED MOTHER

Dear Blessed Mother Mary, I ask you this day to take my child/ren under your protective mantle to guide and protect from any evil influence and harm. Please inspire my child/ren to seek holiness, living virtuous lives so that they will be pleasing to our Lord, your Son, Jesus Christ. Amen.

A MOTHER'S PRAYER
TO THE BLESSED MOTHER

Dear Blessed Mother Mary, you knew the importance of being prayerful and also of being attentive to one's family. Please teach me how to do both well. Please bring me closer to your son, Jesus. Because my vocation of motherhood keeps me very involved with the task at hand, please give me reminders as I go about my day to raise my heart and mind to God often, asking for help and grace. Please keep my family under your powerful protection. Amen.

FOUR

A Mother's Prayerful Life

Prayer to be fruitful must come from the heart and must be able to touch the heart of God.

— Blessed Teresa of Calcutta

St. Frances of Rome, a wife and mother, said, "It is most laudable in a married woman to be devout, but she must never forget that she is a housewife and sometimes must leave God at the altar to find him in housekeeping."

Please, don't be offended! Most wives and mothers don't want to be referred to as "housewives." We are not married to our houses, after all. Mothers don't want to be thought of as only capable of housework! St. Frances of Rome, I am sure, only wished to emphasize the fact that God has given mothers a very important, awesome task — an extremely sublime mission! Yes, we need to become holy, yet we need to achieve that holiness in the midst of our family, even when we may desire to achieve it elsewhere, especially in holy places. Holiness, however, is found in our homes, our "domestic churches."

We can attend Mass, participate in public devotions, and make visits to the Blessed Sacrament where Jesus awaits us. When our children are young, though, mothers usually pray at home in dealing with and caring for the family.

Duty calls constantly. Moms are on call twenty-four hours a day, seven days a week. I don't think we'll have any disagreement here. So we learn to make our life a prayer.

I had the opportunity to stay at a Missionaries of Charity convent in Harlem, New York, to help in the soup kitchen and participate in prayers and daily life with the sisters. Each time the sisters were to go to the chapel for prayer, a bell rang drawing them together. I thought about the similarities between a nun's prayer life and a mother's prayer life as I prayed in the chapel. Just as the bell ringing in the convent calls the sisters to the chapel for prayer, so our family calling for dinner, our baby crying to be nursed, and all our family's other needs "ring" our bell for prayer in service.

At home, if time allows, moms can kneel for their morning and evening prayers and take some time to meditate on Scripture. Prayer is very good, and very necessary. But try to tell a wailing child that he or she has to wait for help because Mommy has decided to kneel down to pray first! Likewise, families are not going to want to exercise patience waiting for dinner because Mommy decided to lock herself in her room to pray and meditate. I am sure you get the picture! A mother knows when the time is right to pray formally and when she is needed.

Mothers have to find a proper balance for prayer on their knees and prayer in action. A dedicated and prayerful mother will realize that by tending to her children's needs, she is truly pleasing our Lord. Just as Blessed Teresa of Calcutta saw Jesus' face in the faces of all the poor and suffering, a mother sees her Lord's face in the faces of her own offspring.

✑ *Personal Prayer: Our Life Is a Prayer*

Love cannot remain by itself — it has no meaning. Love has to be put into action, and that action is service. How do we put the love for God into action? By being faithful to our family, to the duties that God has entrusted to us.
— Blessed Teresa of Calcutta

By God's grace, a mother makes her life a prayer. We start our day, when we open our eyes with the Morning Offering or our own conversation with God, offering our day to him. This starts the day with the proper disposition. When we pray like this, each of our prayers, works, joys, and sufferings throughout the day are thus offered to the Lord. We begin each day with a prayer, which is of no little significance.

"Dear Lord Jesus, thank you for this new day, a new opportunity to serve you in my family. Help me, please to be open to your love and grace for me today. Help me to find the joy in my vocation even when I am feeling tired and challenged, so I will have peace in my heart and may radiate that joy and peace to others."

Personal prayer is essential for a mother to have the strength to carry out her never-ending tasks in the home. But how can we find time for personal prayer?

Any mother will attest that there never seem to be enough hours in the day. Spare time seems to be a luxury reserved for others. Housework is never finished. Laundry piles up forever, dishes seem to multiply in the sink, and the dust settles everywhere! And the care of the children is all-consuming.

To attempt to set aside a special "quiet" time for prayer is nearly impossible. Most times, it *is* impossible! Instead, as mothers we learn that our life *becomes* a prayer. Our entire day and oftentimes our nights are filled with many selfless, loving, sacrificing services for our family. We offer everything to the Lord with love.

St. Catherine of Siena said, "You must pray the prayer of action, which is the fragrant flower of the soul. A good man [woman] is a prayer."

Though we may organize our time to be more efficient, this will help only to a certain extent, especially when we have babies and little ones demanding our undivided attention. Most children's issues need immediate addressing. Crises and emergencies can crop up at any time, as can fatigue. This is when flexibility must come in.

Throughout the difficulties in trying to find the time for prayer, we can persevere even if it is in bits and pieces. Our Lord knows our hearts. He will reward a mother's efforts and will watch over our families. Our Lord wants the bits and pieces of our hearts.

Blessed Teresa of Calcutta taught us that "Prayer to be fruitful must come from the heart and must be able to touch the heart of God. See how Jesus taught his disciples to pray. Call God your Father, praise and glorify his name. Do his will, ask for daily bread, spiritual and temporal; ask for forgiveness of your own sins and that we may forgive others — and also for the grace to be delivered from evil which is in and around us." Simple, succinct, and appropriate advice for all mothers to follow.

So from our hearts as we go about our motherly duties, we pray to touch the heart of God, by lifting up to him our actions of love and service to our families. He knows we are busy! He made us the moms! He knows that we can't stop everything and drop to our knees to pray. He wants us to pray throughout our daily actions.

Pray to remember to lift your heart to God often. He is there to listen. He is waiting. He wants us to satiate his thirst on the Cross, by opening our hearts and lifting them to him. He is very pleased when a mother offers her heart to him in the midst of her hurried day. Strive to find the opportunities to do just that.

We can say decades of the rosary, one at a time during the course of the day — while nursing a baby, chauffeuring our children to their various activities, cleaning the house, and washing the dishes. We can pray through all of our daily routines. Our ten fingers can become a substitute for a decade of the rosary when our hands are occupied with our motherly chores.

Sometimes every bit of our mental capacity is being used to manage the job at hand with the children. Our Lord does know our hearts and does know that we want to come closer to him. He also knows that we need to focus on our children. They depend on us for their safety and well-being. He knows that we are doing just exactly what he has asked us to do. So when our minds are preoccupied with "stuff" that we have to do or are doing, we can ask our Lord if our heart can remain with him as we go about our duties.

From time to time we can offer up little prayers, little conversations with the Divine. We can say, "Dear Lord, Jesus, I love you — be with me, please, and with my family. Help me to teach my children well. Help me to draw others to you by my love and example. Please give me courage, strength, and grace as I go about my day caring for the family that you have entrusted to me. Please open my heart more fully to you."

We can speak to Mary as we say, "Dear Mother Mary, help me to imitate your love and tenderness, help me to be the kind of mother our Lord wants me to be. Inspire me, and grace me please with love and patience. Pray for me to receive our Lord's graces into my heart, and please protect my family."

Another practice that mothers can do at home is to pray to receive a spiritual communion since we cannot receive Jesus in Holy Communion at home. We can pray a short prayer, lifting our hearts to God and asking that we can receive Jesus spiritually. Although we might wish we could be at Mass more often or kneeling before Jesus in the Blessed Sacrament, we are right where God has put us, right where we should be.

Blessing ourselves with the Sign of the Cross often during the day is an additional way to lift our hearts to God. Even if we cannot think of a prayer to follow the blessing, the Sign of the Cross will suffice as a prayer and a protection. It is also a remembrance of our Lord's Passion. We will remain in prayer throughout the day. All of these practices will help to bring us closer to our Lord and will keep us in communication with him.

A parental blessing can be imparted on our children. When they are leaving for school or when we are tucking them in at night and after prayers are said and a good-night kiss and hug, the Sign of the Cross can be traced on their foreheads, with our thumb or finger, while praying for God to bless them. Yes, parents can give a blessing!

After a long day, we can finally get on our knees and give thanks to God formally, during our evening prayers for all his generous blessings. We can ask forgiveness for our shortcomings and grace to improve, to serve our Lord and our family even more lovingly tomorrow.

And after we flop into our bed at night we can be comforted knowing we have done our best to stay in communication with our Lord throughout our busy day. We have tried to pass on the best of ourselves to our family. Pope John Paul II spoke about a mother's daily heroism in his encyclical *Evangelium Vitae* when he wrote of "the silent but effective and eloquent witness of all those brave mothers who devote themselves to their own family without reserve, who suffer in giving birth to their children and who are ready to make any effort, to face any sacrifice, in order to pass on to them the best of themselves." Thank you, dear Pope John Paul II for those words of affirmation that go straight to a mother's heart and help us feel as heroes to our families!

✌ *To the Ends of the Earth*

Pope John Paul II and Pope Benedict XVI have urged the laity to live out their Christianity, their communion with Christ by taking the message of the gospel "to the ends of the earth." Pope Benedict reminded us that the Apostles were the first to tread the steps of Jesus' ministry of evangelization all over the world. At the Sea of Galilee, Jesus had called Simon, Andrew, James, and John "fishers of men."

"The Apostles' adventure began as an encounter between people who opened to one another," Pope Benedict explained. He added that because they had a direct knowledge of the Master, they were "witnesses to the person of Christ." not just "proclaiming an idea."

Because the Apostles had a personal relationship with Jesus they were able to accurately and articulately convey Jesus to those they met. If they hadn't developed that intimate friendship with Jesus they would not have been able to pass on the true and entire message of Christ to others. It would have been only nice words or good intentions.

In the same way, if we are to evangelize through our encounters and relationships with people — in our families, in the workplace and in the community, we must deepen our relationship with our Lord first, so that we will be bringing his message, to the ends of the earth, not a watered down version or our own interpretation.

Reaching the ends of the earth is begun in our own hearts. We deepen our prayer lives and strive to come closer to our Lord. We make use of the sacraments as often as is possible to infuse our souls with truth and light. Our intimate relationship with Jesus compels us to continue his ministry on earth as the Apostles did.

Blessed Teresa of Calcutta preached the gospel by doing, by living it. She seldom preached to the masses. The majority of her preaching was within her ministry, to one person at a time. She did not preach Christ's message shouting from the rooftops, but through her loving hands and her selfless heart to each person she met as she lived an utter testament to the gospel. Yet the gospel that was lived through her to one person at a time made it to the ends of the earth.

Mothers too, are called to continue Christ's message of love, of repentance, of forgiveness, of mercy, and of everlasting life. Our evangelization will occur each and every day to the extent that we are willing to live the gospel. Realizing that our actions are many times much more articulate than our words can ever be, we must consider our responses to everything and everyone that fills our days.

Additionally, we have to decide if we will go about our days with grumbling and complaining about our circumstances and situations, or with a joy that will radiate out to others and attract them to the blessedness of our Christianity. "Joy is a net to catch souls," Blessed Teresa always used to say. Are we catching souls by our lives of love and joy?

In our lives, maybe evangelizing to "the ends of the earth" actually means the ends of the household. But when we all follow in our Lord's footsteps, our households will be transformed and the souls in our families will be converted by God's grace.

To the ends of the earth, to the ends of the household, let us be fishers of men with our nets of love and joy!

✍ *Hugs and Giggles!*

> *Be joyful always.*
> — 1 Thessalonians 5:16

We delight in the happy times of play with our children. These playful times together with our brood are also a prayer. Sometimes when our children want us to play with them, it seems difficult or impossible to drop the housework we are up to our elbows with for fear we may never finish. Yet we should oblige our children, taking the time to be with them and play with them. They are growing older each day. Before long they won't want to play with us; they will be too busy with other activities and with their friends.

Our life with our children *is* a prayer. Children need a well-rounded home life. And play is an important and joyful part of it. When older, our children will have had the wealth of many fun childhood experiences and heartfelt memories to recall and reminisce about and even pass down to their own children.

Seize the opportunity. Leave the work and go out and shoot some hoops with your children. Throw that Frisbee or softball with them. Take a nice stroll and admire nature, or play a board game with them. Revel in your enjoyment with them. And yes, it's all right to splash through the puddles on your bicycles together, jump in the leaf piles, or make snow angels. Lighten up and have some fun. This together time is valuable. It will also bring us closer to our children.

We can read to our children, too, especially inspirational stories, stories emphasizing good morals and values, and books on the lives of the saints and other holy people. Our home must be the place where our children will learn the truth about God and their faith. They certainly will hear plenty from outside influences that will contradict our teachings, sad to say. If we have started early with prayer and teaching, our children will have a strong foundation to stand firm and unshaken against the attacks from the world.

Throughout our children's lives, we must work to always keep the lines of communication open. We must learn to become good listeners. "Patience" becomes our middle name! As they grow, in addition to sharing their happy moments with us, our children will feel comfortable turning to us in times of stress or difficulties if we have shown them that we care enough to listen well.

Sometimes we feel caught up in a whirlwind of work and have trouble focusing on our children. Let's try to take a breath, slow down, and enjoy our family.

When our children are young, we cannot expect to check off everything on our "To Do" lists. Unexpected things are forever coming up. But children's needs should take precedence. Let's take some time to giggle and play without guilt, and let's not forget those back tickles!

✑ Teach Them to Give

Another prayerful part of our journey is teaching our children to give, to reach out of themselves and serve family members and their neighbor. Our self-centered world isn't exactly conducive to giving of ourselves. Our children are never too young to learn this important practice. And they observe us in our dealings with others.

The time of year prior to Christmas is an ideal time to teach our young ones to think of other people's needs and learn the true gift that giving really is. It is usually a "gimme, gimme, I want, I want" time for them. Teaching children to see past themselves is vital.

Together with our children, we can come up with all kinds of ways to give. Our little ones can help us decorate Christmas cookies to be given to a needy family or the local soup kitchen. Cards and letters can be written to families in need because of natural disasters, war, or poverty. We can volunteer at our local soup kitchen with our older children one day a month, or possibly invite members of our parish to join us. We can visit a local elderly housing community on a regular basis and become friendly with the residents. We can volunteer to arrange a social event occasionally at one of these communities. Area nursing homes can always use some friendly faces to help cheer patients who do not have friends or relatives nearby. The list of possibilities is endless.

Remember that love and care are needed year round, not just around the holidays when many organizations plan annual outreach events or drives. We can come up with giving opportunities of our own by taking our family's ideas, throwing in lots of love, and stirring together for an original family recipe for giving!

In guiding our children to become more prayerful and give of themselves while they are young, we are teaching them the way to get through the narrow gate. We don't want them to wander in the wrong direction in what is disguised as an easier or better path, since we know "The gate is wide and the road broad that leads to destruction." (Matthew 7:13)

The Importance of a Loving Touch

While raising our children, we need to remember that though they absolutely need our love and physical affection, they may not always appreciate the way we tender it. Our young ones may be "too busy" for a hug or a kiss, and our preteens and teenagers may pull away. Whatever the age, there's no need to give up our attempts to show them affection.

No one is too old or too big for a hug or a kiss. Haven't psychologists told us that for emotional survival alone we need at least four hugs a day?

I believe it all starts in the womb — with the warm amniotic fluid caressing a baby's skin, cushioning him while his mother rocks him gently with her every move. A baby is accustomed to comfort and affection right from the start.

We emerge into this world wanting to be comforted after a strenuous birth process. The world outside the womb is very different from our first warm, dark, and safe environment. A baby may cry because he's hungry or uncomfortable, and he may also cry because he's lonely and needs physical contact. Sometimes a simple touch or caress, such as a hand on your baby's back, will soothe a fussy baby. At other times, he will need to be picked up, rocked, cuddled, or walked to satisfy him and stop his fretful crying.

Babies cannot be spoiled by love. When a baby cries for comfort and physical contact and is left in his crib and not picked up, he will learn to be distrustful and may feel that this world must be an awful place. However, each time we fulfill our baby's cravings for affection, we have helped to establish his sense of confidence, trust, and happiness in his new world.

In the eighteenth century, Frederick II of Prussia conducted a very unusual experiment. He came up with a crazy scheme to discover mankind's original language. He instructed the nurses and caretakers at an orphanage to feed and change the babies there, taking care of only their physical needs. They were absolutely forbidden to talk to the babies in the hope that the babies would, on their own, come out with their first language without any outside influence.

The babies were left in their cribs without receiving any attention between feedings. The nurses did not hold the babies and did not speak at all in their presence. There was no show of affection. The tragic outcome to this crazy experiment was that all of the babies died! They were psychologically starved.

The human touch is a very positive and crucial part of growing up and developing into healthy, stable human beings. Children need to feel loved, and they need to feel that love in a physical way.

At times, throughout the various phases of development, our children may pull away from or become embarrassed by our signs of affection toward them, especially when it is given in front of friends. Not to worry, these phases will pass. And they may quietly welcome our hug or kiss at another more opportune moment.

Today's ever-busier world with its extremely hectic pace leaves little time for cuddling. As mothers, we need to make a point of placing importance on inviting our children to be with us by sitting them on our laps when they run in from school, giving them a big hug, encouraging them to talk — even if only for a few minutes — about their day. Such closeness, supported by our love, helps to prepare them for their next adventure.

Nothing can come close to a parent's shoulder for a child to put her head upon when she wants a little comfort. This essential physical touch can be given when we read our youngsters a story. Holding hands during a walk, playing a game with them in a physical way, or rocking our infants are other examples of simple ways we can physically show our love. Showing affection is very fundamental and vital to our children's well-being. It also prepares our youngsters to express affection later in their own lives. So, let's not be shy with those hugs and kisses!

SEEKING PERSEVERANCE, TRUST, AND A NEW HEART

Heavenly Father, please grant me a new heart. Thank you for the many blessings of every day, blessings I sometimes don't recognize. Help me to realize that when obstacles seem to get in the path of prayer, I should not give in to discouragement or give up my efforts on prayer, even during dry periods. Help me to empty my heart of all the clutter that gets in the way of coming closer to you. Please grant me the graces to persevere in prayer with trust and humility in my pursuit of unity with you. I beg you to speak to the silence of my heart as I seek to quench your thirst for souls. Help me to find the opportune moments to gaze upon you as I go about my many tasks of mothering so that I may come closer to you while I strive to bring my family to you. Amen.

HELP ME TO
TEACH MY CHILDREN WELL

Dear Lord Jesus, you have given me an awesome and sometimes overwhelming task, a job like no other. When I brought my children into this world, I took on the responsibility to teach them well and steer them away from all that will hurt their souls. It is not easy, in the environment of our technological world today, to have control over all that may influence my children negatively. I pray for your grace, insight, wisdom, and strength to continue in my mission as mother and teacher. Amen.

F I V E

Family Prayer

Prayer is joy, prayer is love, and prayer is peace. You cannot explain it; you must experience prayer. It is not impossible. God gives it for the asking.

— Blessed Teresa of Calcutta

Blessed Teresa of Calcutta was forever saying, "A family that prays together, stays together." We know this is true. Common prayer unites our minds, hearts, and souls. There is less fighting and disunity in a prayerful home. The household will ring with laughter and merriment, and peace will dwell within. Who am I trying to fool? Between the children's bickering, that is!

But, honestly, prayer will keep us together, even in the midst of problems, confusion, or difficulties. Because a prayerful family has a solid foundation in its faith, during trying times a family will turn to prayer naturally. The graces from this will certainly enable the family to persevere.

We live in an era where broken families and families not at peace are the norm rather than the exception. Pope John Paul II told us that we are "at a moment of history in which the family is the object of numerous forces that seek to destroy it or in some way to deform it" (*Familiaris Consortio*). We must not take his words lightly.

Life in a family is not always accommodating. Therefore, we need to consciously find time to pray together. We need to ask our Lord for his help and his grace to remain prayerful people. Ideally, prayer is a holy experience, a peaceful, quiet time. While we must not be demanding or forceful about prayer, we should encourage prayer on a regular basis when our children are small, though it will be difficult to keep them very still or quiet for long. Our Lord knows that they are children and that they will learn in time. Flexibility and patience are paramount.

ᓚᔓ *Prayer at Church*

There will be times when we can bring our little ones before the Lord, before Jesus in the Blessed Sacrament where he awaits our visits. We can stop by the church when we are out and about doing errands. We can go in and genuflect and kneel down for just a few minutes with our children. There we will receive the grace and strength to carry out our duties. We will receive amazing peace to continue on our journey. Our hearts will be filled with more of Christ's love, grace, and guidance.

We should also remember that even our small children receive graces during holy Mass. Even when it is difficult for us to participate, or at times to actually hear what is happening at Mass, our Lord is pleased that we have brought our "little ones" to him. He tells us, "Let the little children come to me, and do not hinder them, for of such is the kingdom of God. Amen I say to you, whoever does not accept the kingdom of God as a little child will not enter into it."

We should try not to be hurt or offended if we receive a stare at Mass from someone not particularly appreciating our children. Let us muster up a smile in return for the glare; God bless you!

I will never forget my first encounter with Blessed Teresa of Calcutta, not just because I considered her to be a living saint, but because of what she said to me. My family and I were attending a Mass with the sisters at a Missionary of Charity convent located in Washington, D.C. I felt extra cognizant of the fact that I was bringing my three children, Justin, Chaldea, and Jessica into a very quiet chapel.

Jessica, my youngest at the time, who was not quite two years old, became fussy during the Mass and started get whiny. I had to take her outside quite a few times during Mass so she wouldn't disturb everyone. After Mass, Mother Teresa came directly up to me as I was holding Jessica and asked me, "Is this the baby who was singing at Mass?" It was so refreshing to hear someone describe a fussy child as "singing," especially since it was Mother Teresa! We were also surprised when Mother Teresa ran across the room to give a great big hug to my six-year-old daughter, Chaldea. Mother Teresa had spotted Chaldea genuflecting very beautifully in front of the Blessed Sacrament on her own before leaving the chapel and Mother appeared to be touched by my daughter's faithful action.

✍ Each New Day

Pope Paul VI expressed the importance of family prayer when he said, "The unity and security of the family will find their sure defense and unfailing protection in the practice of family prayer. As the motto of the Family Rosary Crusade succinctly asserts: 'We therefore warmly recommend the practice of daily prayer, of family prayer, and of prayer by means of the rosary.'" Pope John Paul II expressed a similar thought when he said, "There is no doubt that the rosary should be considered as one of the best and most efficacious prayers in common that the Christian family is invited to recite."

Mothers should teach their children to pray from an early age. Prayer, then, will come as naturally to them as breathing. Little aspirations, vocalized in our children's presence, such as "Thank you, dear Lord, for this day, a new day to spread your love and do your will," will help our children to be thankful for each new day and to understand that prayer can be said at any time. It is a conversation with God, not a burden or a weighty obligation. The importance of prayer in a family cannot be underestimated. By praying with and in front of our children, from an early age, we will lay down a very important foundation that will remain with them throughout life.

We know that it is our duty to teach our children to pray. Pope John Paul II reminded us of this when he said, "By reason of their dignity and mission, Christian parents have the specific responsibility of educating their children in prayer, introducing them to gradual discovery of the mystery of God and to personal dialogue with Him."

Therefore, for eternal happiness for the family, a mother needs to develop her own personal prayer life, a family prayer life, and also encourage her children to have their own individual prayer lives.

Each morning as our children are leaving for school or work or play, we can send them off with a Morning Offering and a prayer to their guardian angel, asking for protection and guidance throughout the day.

We should get them in the habit of looking to God when they first wake up to face a new day. We can teach them to thank God for a new day, a fresh start, more blessings, and more chances to spread his love to others. It takes only a moment to drop down to our knees in humility before our Lord. Our children should be taught to take a minute out, no matter how much of a hurry they are in, to greet the Lord at the beginning of a new day. And when they forget, they will know they are welcome to speak to him as soon as they remember.

Being a mother of five children, I know how rushed school mornings can be, trying to get them to eat a good and healthy breakfast, make sure they have everything they need, and get them out the door to catch the bus. In all of the morning madness, if we get our children in the habit of a praying to their guardian angel at the breakfast table, on the way to the bus stop, or on their way to school, we know that their day has begun on the right foot. Morning prayers are an essential habit to develop and will last for a lifetime.

As the mothers of that wonderful group of people God has brought together as our children, we can pray to our children's guardian angels on their behalf — for the little ones too small to voice their own prayers, and later for the older ones no longer under our roofs.

It can take a tremendous effort, at times, to gather your flock for family prayer. It can be rather humorous seeing and hearing the many excuses that can come up at the mention of "prayer time"! Pray for the graces to be faithful to family prayer, whether it is three Hail Mary's together, the Angelus, the rosary, an Our Father or whatever. Pope John Paul II said it doesn't matter how you pray just so long as you pray!

Keep in mind that the forces of evil that never rest are always at work attempting to interfere with or stop family prayer. All of the graces are available to us. It's amazing how we can make the time for other things such as a meeting, a television program, a phone call, an appointment, a playdate, or a shopping trip. Why not a meeting with the Lord? We need to place importance on prayer, which is really so necessary for the survival of a happy and healthy family.

Around the Dinner Table, a Holy Time

The family above all — is the special place of the human person, it provides the environment in which the person is conceived, is born and grows — the context of the person's earthly happiness and human hope.

— Pope John Paul II

At the dinner table, after grace is said, we can say a Hail Mary united as a family. Our Blessed Mother will be honored and will protect our families. We can say an Our Father, as well. I find that the dinner table is a perfect place for family prayer, since we have a captive audience! It is wise to get everyone in the habit of praying before eating while they are still hungry, rather than afterward, when everyone has something "very important" to do, *immediately!*

Dinnertime, is a great time to regroup and reconnect as a family, generally sharing stories about our day, talking over tomorrow's plans, praising our children for their accomplishments, and just relaxing and enjoying each other's company. Something very special and holy happens when a family gathers together. Our children will look back when they are older and reminisce about those happy times around the dinner table. We mothers should do our best to safeguard this special time.

Life speeds by, and there are many distractions pulling us away from this holy time. Phone calls, TV, the Internet, homework, and other activities can wait for a short time. There isn't a lot of time in our day when we can all sit down and just be together. Very few families these days have regular family meals, and we know how rushed mornings are. Take advantage of that wonderful together time.

Sports games, practices, and after-school activities sometimes run into evening family time. Although these can be great occasions for individual family members and for supporting each other, we need to make sure that these activities, however wholesome they may be, don't take over our lives entirely, or rob our family dinners! We have to set limits as befit our family's best interests.

Along with eating dinner together, family nights can be planned for one night a week. This works well for families with older children. Dinner may be followed by a board game, movie, or an outdoor activity, weather permitting, or whatever other activity the family enjoys. These enjoyable times become a memorable part of our family traditions.

Family experiences are important in raising our children. Pope John Paul II has told us that family experiences will strongly condition the attitudes that children will assume as adults. He said, "Children very soon learn about life. They watch and imitate the behavior of adults. They rapidly learn love and respect for others, but they also quickly absorb the poison of violence and hatred. Family experiences strongly condition the attitudes that children will assume as adults. Consequently, if the family is the place where children first encounter the world, the family must be for children the first school of peace."

We don't have to look very far around us to see the effects on our society simply because prayer was not taught to children or they did not have the benefit of a peaceful, loving family environment.

Our dinner tables and our homes are safe havens, places of refreshment and refuge for all of our family members. We should keep them loving, uplifting, and even holy.

✒ *Together in Prayer*

A good reason for teaching children to pray while they are young is so they develop the habit of prayer before they grow older and feel they don't have time or a desire for it.

By saying at least one Hail Mary together as a family, we are united in prayer and honoring our Blessed Mother together, and that is a very good thing.

When we are together in prayer, while sitting or kneeling, we can encourage each family member to form a prayer petition or a prayer of thanksgiving. In this way, children learn to express themselves to God through prayer, being thankful for all that God has given us and praying for those who are less fortunate than us. A selected decade of the rosary or other family prayers may be said with the prayer petitions for all those who have asked for our prayers. Let us not forget to pray for the poor souls in purgatory who need our prayers and will reward us with theirs.

↜ *At the End of the Day*

Tucking in each child at night is a great time to have them pray to their guardian angel. With our child we can thank our Lord for his blessings and love, as well as for protecting our household and any siblings who live away from home.

St. Louis de Montfort in *The Secret of the Rosary* said, "Pray with great confidence based upon the goodness and infinite generosity of God and upon the promises of Jesus Christ. God is a spring of living water, which flows unceasingly into the hearts of those who pray. The eternal Father yearns for nothing so much as to share the life-giving waters of his grace and mercy with us. He is entreating us: 'All you that thirst, come to the waters.'"

As mothers, we need to pray "with great confidence," remembering to ask our Lord Jesus and his Blessed Mother Mary for all the graces we need to carry out the many tasks of motherhood and for special grace to gather our family together again and again for prayer, where we will constantly be nourished at the "spring of living water" that our Lord is calling us to.

PRAYER FOR A NEW DAY

Beloved Hearts of Jesus and Mary, I offer you my prayers, works, joys, and sufferings of this day, praying that all that I do may be worthy of your love. Help me to be open to hear the cries of those in need. Please give me the grace to be kind and merciful to them. Help me to be always open to the needs right here under my own roof. I offer all I am and all I do for the salvation of souls, the reunion of all Christians, the grace of repentance, and the intentions of our Holy Father. I wish to unite my heart with yours and make my life this day a prayer. Amen.

BLESS OUR DOMESTIC CHURCH

Oh, Lord, you have blessed me with the sacred gift of the family. You have put my children in my care to raise in a loving home. Whether we live in a palace or under a tree, we are a family. You bless our comings and goings, our times together and times apart when we look to you for grace and love. Help me to see the sacred beauty in my domestic church where many of my prayers are voiced to you throughout the care of my family and household. Please continue to strengthen me and give me peace in my vocation. Bless us all this day, Lord, as we live together, pray together, eat together, and work together in the blessedness of our family. Amen.

SIX

Saintly Mothers

✤❦✤

A woman's dignity is closely connected with the love which she receives by the very reason of her femininity; it is likewise connected with the love which she gives in return.
— Pope John Paul II,
Mulieris Dignitatem

We can be certain that Heaven is filled with saints who were once mothers on earth. A priest I know, Father Bill C. Smith, says with a smile, "Good, faithful mothers skip purgatory and go straight to Heaven!"

Although there's no question that a mother immensely enjoys rearing her children, her role is actually a sacrificial one. Her time and energies focus on her children. We know that our Lord will reward her efforts and love and that her children will be the jewels on her crown in eternity!

A mother's vocation — to conceive and bring eternal souls into this world so they may work out their salvation — is awesome. Everything else will eventually turn to dust, but the fruit of a mother's labors will live on eternally! Our Lord surely has favored mothers, entering into a partnership with them to create human life. In a sense, both our Lord and our mom have the same job: to bring souls to the salvation of Heaven.

We can learn a great deal from the saints that will surely help us on our own journeys. A few of their stories follow.

✍ *St. Monica*

When reading about St. Monica, we learn that she faced some difficulties that are similar to those modern-day mothers must contend with. Monica's husband did not believe in God. Her eldest son, Augustine, although brilliant, was wasting his life, in his mother's opinion, since he was living in sin. Augustine was living with a woman and had an illegitimate son. St. Monica was very concerned about the fact that her son had also been indoctrinated into a strange religious cult and had become a Manichean.

Both Monica's husband and son seemed to turn a deaf ear to her pleadings and her living example to them as a woman of faith. St. Monica was left to depend on prayer alone for the conversions of her husband and son. She would often plead with our Lord through her many tears, begging for divine assistance.

St. Monica confided in a bishop when she was worried about her wayward son, Augustine. He acknowledged the power of a mother's prayers when he said, "Go your way! As sure as you live, it is impossible that the son of a mother with these tears should perish." The bishop was certain that God would never turn his ear from Monica's pleadings and tears.

St. Monica persevered in prayer. It's what she knew, what her heart told her to do. She refused to give up. God gave her the grace and understanding to know that her family's salvation depended on her fervent and continuous prayer. Of course, this took much sacrifice on her part and a very strong determination to remain steadfast in her faith and in her prayer.

In time, Monica's intense prayer and sacrifice paid off. This prayerful woman's husband converted and was baptized before his death, and Augustine not only changed his sinful ways, he miraculously began to lead a very holy and exemplary life. The Church has declared both Augustine and his mother, Monica, to be saints. It's amazing what prayer can do and continues to do down through the ages.

Every mother needs to grab onto that truth and apply it to her own life. God may allow us to be in very difficult or seemingly impossible situations in our lives to help bring about our sanctity and that of our family through our faithful, loving, and persistent prayer.

If we keep in mind that the words spoken to St. Monica must certainly be words meant for all mothers, we will find consolation and peace. Our Lord couldn't possibly turn his ear from the prayers of a faithful, prayerful mother. We must never forget that. Mothers should never give up on hope. We will certainly never hope in vain as long as we remain prayerful.

Dear St. Monica, please find it in your heart to also pray for us mothers here on Earth for the strength and grace to continue on our journey. Oh, dear Lord Jesus, please continue to hear the prayers of mothers all around the world who are pleading for help for their families!

✐ *St. Elizabeth Ann Seton*

Life didn't seem fair to Betty Ann Bayley, later known to us as St. Elizabeth Seton. Her mother died when she was just three years old. When her father remarried, he ignored Elizabeth and her sisters. After some time, her father separated from his second wife. The children went to live with an aunt and uncle for about six years.

Elizabeth, who was brought up Episcopalian, grew up as a lonely child. Because of her loneliness she may have been more inclined to seek God, whom she came to know through nature and her church. As a teen, she read her Bible a great deal.

Even though her life was sad at times, Elizabeth never became bitter. Fortunately, Elizabeth's father eventually returned Elizabeth's affection, and their relationship became stable and loving again.

Elizabeth fell in love with William Seton and was married in January 1794. Her life became filled with beautiful things. She became a magnificent wife and mother, and she enjoyed caring for her house. She was filled with great joy, knowing that she was pleasing our Lord with her many acts of love and service to her children.

Over the years, misfortune seemed to knock at her door. Her family fell into financial ruin. Serious illnesses struck one family member after another. However, the adversity gave her an opportunity to grow in faith and to mature in character, and her spirituality deepened through prayer.

Elizabeth cared for her family lovingly and still found time to nurse sick friends. There is an interesting story about Elizabeth's conversion to the Catholic faith. She had to travel to Italy with her daughter Ann Marie and her very ill husband, Will, hoping for a cure for his tuberculosis.

She faced many difficulties there in the cold, damp, bare room where they stayed. Despite their efforts to save Will, sadly he died. Anne Marie and Elizabeth had to remain in Italy for several months after Will's death because they were quarantined when a bout of scarlet fever prevented their departure.

Although Elizabeth was homesick and missed her other children terribly, she realized God's purpose through it all in detaining her as she became certain and convinced of the truth of Catholicism.

Elizabeth and her daughter finally sailed home to New York and met her other children and her sister there when their boat docked. Elizabeth was hit with yet another blow when she found out about her dear sister-in-law's tuberculosis.

Elizabeth wavered in her decision to embrace Catholicism, disheartened by the way family and friends reacted to her changed religious attitude. In time, though, in addition to converting to Catholicism, she went on to found the first American order of religious sisters, and afterward she opened the first parochial school in America.

Elizabeth took her vocation as a mother very seriously, always putting her children first and foremost. Without hesitation, she put her own personal concerns and desires second. Her children were always corrected lovingly, although firmly. She was successful at keeping the lines of communication open with her children.

St. Elizabeth Seton is a fine example of holiness in a laywoman who was also a mother. The tapestry of her life was woven with many joys and sorrows. Throughout her life's trials, she remained faithful to God. She possessed a deep inner conviction to pray and to even deepen her prayer life to survive. We know that we, too, often experience discomfort due to the feelings of abandonment and ostracism we face as well.

Though we may not achieve such great accomplishments as Elizabeth by God's grace was able to, such as opening up convents and schools, we experience similar joys and sorrows. God will, though, expect us to carry out our motherly duties as wholeheartedly and faithfully as we are able to, even throughout our trials and tribulations.

We can strive to imitate Elizabeth's virtues, knowing that she too was a mother. She is a wonderful example of holiness in a mother. We can pray for the grace to be faithful to God in all our life's joys and sorrows. In so doing, we will bring grace to our families and set a beautiful example for others, bringing many to our Lord.

Dear St. Elizabeth Seton, look fondly on us mothers who live in a different time and a seemingly different world than you did. Though time has separated us, our prayers to the same God unite us. Please pray to our Lord Jesus for us so we may imitate you and become virtuous mothers!

ᴄᴏ *St. Rita of Cascia*

St. Rita of Cascia was also a mother. Before she was conceived, her parents had prayed long and hard for a child. Rita was born in May of 1381. She had a happy childhood and was prayerful even as a child. A desire to become a cloistered religious seemed to have been instilled in her heart, but her parents refused her requests. They chose a husband for her instead. Rita gave up her innermost desire to become a nun and consented obediently to her parents' wishes.

Rita married a man who unfortunately possessed a violent temper. He was very cruel at times to Rita. Rita practiced many heroic virtues, offering her sufferings to the Lord. She had two sons who began to follow in their father's footsteps, imitating his angry traits and characteristics. Sadly, they became cold and ungrateful toward their mother. Rita knew in her heart that she needed to increase her prayers and make many sacrifices for the good of her family. Miraculously, her husband, in time, converted and became an upright Christian man.

One evening, her husband was murdered on his way home from work. Being the holy woman that she was, even though Rita felt shattered about her loss, her thoughts turned immediately to concerns over whether he had died without the last sacraments. It is said that God revealed to Rita that her husband's soul was saved.

The tragedy of her husband's death didn't bring bitterness to Rita's heart, but rather, remarkably, she felt forgiveness toward his murderer. Her sons, however, were determined to seek revenge. Fearing the repercussions of their impending sins, St. Rita stormed Heaven with prayer, valiantly begging our Lord to even take her sons to himself if that was needed to prevent them from committing such a grave sin.

God answered her prayer. The boys fell ill. They had time to reflect on their intentions and to change their minds and hearts during their illnesses. They both died peacefully less than a year after their father's death.

Rita courageously put her sons' salvation ahead of her own natural motherly desires to be with her children. She sacrificed immensely for them. She was left alone but with a peaceful heart.

The religious life beckoned her again, now that she was alone and without family responsibilities. She wanted to be admitted to the Augustinian monastery but was refused because she was a widow. It is said that she entered miraculously, however, through a bolted door with the assistance of John the Baptist, Augustine, and Nicholas of Tolentino.

She voluntarily led a penitential life in the monastery, imitating Jesus. During Lent in 1443, she listened intently to St. James of Marche preach on Christ's passion. Rita was greatly moved, and upon returning to the convent, she knelt before a crucifix, begging God to share with her at least part of his pains.

A thorn from the crown of thorns was loosened miraculously and fell and was planted deeply into Rita's forehead. Overcome with pain, Rita fainted. The wound remained.

In 1450, declared a holy year by the pope, Rita asked to accompany the nuns on a pilgrimage to Rome. Her superior told her that she could go if her wound healed. Rita asked our Lord to cure the wound but let the pain continue. The grace was granted. She traveled to Rome, and upon arriving home, her wound reopened.

Three years later, Rita developed a serious illness, confining her to bed for the remainder of her life. Her body deteriorated and she longed for Heaven. She received the last sacraments and asked forgiveness from her community of nuns. She promised that she would remember them all in Heaven.

On May 22, 1457, Rita went home to Heaven at the age of seventy-six. Her death was crowned with miracles. The monastery bells rang without human assistance at the moment of her death. Her deteriorated face became transformed and radiant. The wound on her forehead glowed. A holy fragrance surrounded her.

Soon pilgrimages made their way to her famed tomb. Devotion to her spread throughout the world. Rita of Cascia became universally acclaimed as the Saint of the Impossible, and Pope Leo XIII canonized her in 1900. Many invoke St. Rita in desperate times and experience the power of the Saint of the Impossible.

Perhaps we cannot bring ourselves to hope for our children's death, as Rita did, so they would have everlasting life rather than commit a serious crime or sin. Perhaps we cannot imagine such things as Rita longed for or achieved, but God calls us all in our own walks of life and gives us the grace we require to do just exactly what we should do on our own journeys.

Dear St. Rita, please help us to see the holy significance in a mother's sacrifice, and love and pray for us mothers to persevere in our prayers for our families.

✒ *Mothers Are in the Palm of God's Hand*

The saints relied on their faith in God. Their deep prayerful lives increased their faith and got them through the thick and thin. They realized that the times they felt most abandoned by God were when he was in fact carrying them in the palm of his hand!

They learned that their prayer, especially offered to our Lord when they were in turmoil, was so very efficacious to our Lord. With great tenderness, God watched over the women to whom he had entrusted his children. He continues to do so today.

During difficult periods, recall the words spoken to St. Monica: "Go your way! As sure as you live, it is impossible that the son of a mother with these tears should perish." The power of a mother's prayer should never be underestimated.

We must never give up on hope, no matter how far away from the flock our "little" ones will roam. We must be consistent in our prayer for their salvation, remaining faithful and loving and continuing to set a good example.

Blessed Teresa told us that we must have faith to love properly, and that when we love, we can't help but serve, and in doing so, the sacrifice required will bring lasting peace.

A MOTHER'S PRAYER
FOR HER CHILDREN

O Mary, Immaculate Virgin, Mother of our Lord Jesus Christ, patroness of all mothers, I commend my beloved children to the Most Sacred Heart of your son, Jesus, and to your Immaculate Heart. Please assist our family and keep us always in your care. Please protect us from the snares of the devil and keep us on the road that leads to life. Help me to realize my sublime mission as a mother, and help me to be faithful to my duties for the good of my family and the good of the entire family of God.

Most Sacred Heart of Jesus, have mercy on us.
Immaculate Heart of Mary, pray for us.
Holy guardian angel of our family, pray for us.
St. Michael, pray for us.
St. Joseph, husband of Mary, pray for us.
St. Anne, mother of Mary, pray for us.
St. Elizabeth, pray for us.
St. Monica, pray for us.
St. Augustine, pray for us.
St. Gerard Majella, pray for us.
Blessed Mother Teresa of Calcutta, pray for us.
Amen.

ST. JOSEPH, BLESS OUR FAMILY

Dear St. Joseph, I cannot even fathom the feeling you must have had holding baby Jesus in your arms close to your heart. You shepherded your family in great humility, respect, and love. You certainly endured hardship in caring for them. I know in my heart that since God had entrusted the Holy Family to you, he must also entrust all families to you. By your powerful intercession before our Lord, I place my family in your loving embrace. Please hold us close as we journey towards Heaven. Amen.

SEVEN

A Call to Holiness for Mothers

Holiness is not a luxury of a few but a simple duty for you and me, so let us be holy as our Father in Heaven is holy. St. Thomas says, "Sanctity consists in nothing else but a firm resolve," the heroic act of a soul abandoning itself to God." — Blessed Teresa of Calcutta

Why should anyone strive to become a saint in today's world? "Didn't most of the saints live generations before us?" we may ask ourselves. There would probably be too much criticism and ridicule by others, anyway, even from our peers and family if we set out to become holy. We would probably be considered fanatical. How could we fit in? Wouldn't it be impossible to achieve sanctity anyway? After all, isn't saintliness reserved for the very pious, holy, and perfect?

We should know that God calls us all to become holy and saintly. No, saints aren't perfect. They strive for perfection on a daily basis. Becoming holy doesn't mean that we take our halos out of our top dresser drawer each morning, polish them up, and put them on. Saintliness is not pretentious or showy. It is not fanaticism or the practice of some bizarre religious belief. Holiness is actually very natural. It comes from God and requires only a desiring heart and soul. The effects of it radiate outward to others. We are all created to be holy. All of the graces to become holy are available for the asking. Each one of us in our own state of life is called to be holy.

Blessed Teresa of Calcutta constantly professed that holiness is not reserved for a few, but is a duty for everyone. Holiness is really living our lives to our fullest potential within God's will. It is striving to reach our eternal destiny while living in God's providence. It is surrendering our wills to God and praying for the graces to fulfill our duties faithfully.

We are not perfect creatures. We fall many times, even throughout the course of one day. But the difference between a person striving for holiness and one who is indifferent to God's promptings in her soul is that the former will pick herself up, examine her conscience, ask forgiveness for her shortcomings, and strive to improve with prayer.

It is a daily effort: it is an hourly effort. We have to *want* holiness. God will not force it upon us. It is truly a blessed decision to follow God's holy will, utterly and completely.

As we know, our motherly influence, nurturing, and love shapes and molds our impressionable children. By striving for holiness, we are fulfilling our responsibility within our sublime role as a mother.

Mothers are the holy glue that keeps it all together within our families. We are the real heart of our family. Many young eyes look up to us, observing our actions and listening intently to our words, even when we wish they did not!

We will grow in holiness to the extent that we allow God to come into our lives and to the extent that we surrender our wills to him. Through prayer, he will guide us and pour love into our motherly hearts for our children.

"Holiness consists in doing God's will joyfully. Faithfulness makes saints. The spiritual life is a union with Jesus: the divine and the human giving themselves to each other. The only thing Jesus asks of us is to give ourselves to him, in total poverty, and total self-forgetfulness.

"The first step towards holiness is the will to become holy. Through a firm and upright will we love God, we choose God, we hasten to God, we reach him, we have him," Blessed Teresa of Calcutta unambiguously preached.

Giving ourselves to God in total poverty requires emptying our hearts so that we can make room for him. By choosing God and holiness, we can reach him and we can help work out our family's salvation for eternity. Intense food for thought!

To become a saint is really quite simple, according to Blessed Teresa of Calcutta. She lets us in on her secret to holiness: "Very great holiness becomes very simple if we belong fully to Our Lady. Our sanctification is her main duty. She went in haste to help Jesus sanctify John — and so it will be with you and me if we only love her unconditionally and trust her fully. The more we abandon ourselves to her totally and without reserve the more we will be great saints."

Blessed Teresa instructed me to call upon Jesus' Mother and to pray the rosary fervently on many occasions. She told me that our Blessed Mother will absolutely bring me — and all of us — closer to her son.

When describing the canticle of the Magnificat — Mary's response to the Angel Gabriel's announcement that she was chosen to be the mother of the Messiah, recorded in the Gospel of Luke, Pope Benedict XVI said that the first part of the Magnificat is "the celebration of divine grace which irrupted into the heart and the life of Mary, making her Mother of the Lord."

But, he continued explaining, Mary's personal witness was "not solitary because the Virgin Mother was fully aware she had a distinct mission to achieve for humanity, and her own story is part of the history of salvation." Pope Benedict further explained that in the second part of the canticle "the voice of Mary is joined by the entire community of faithful" who celebrate God's actions in history. He also said the Lord "takes the side of the least and the lowliest." We know that throughout history, our Lord has revealed himself to the humble and lowly.

The good news for moms is that while we naturally and lovingly mother our children, we also set a much needed and very important example to our society. And this magnificently comes from us "least and lowly" creatures! We have taken our motherhood seriously and have not let the world's allurements distract us or seduce us into selling our children short.

Our children need us, and we are here for them. We are very thankful for the sacred privilege of motherhood. We pray that the sublime vocation of motherhood will regain its proper dignity and that before long there will be a change in society's attitude toward mothers and the critical role of rearing children. Our children need us; let us truly and wholeheartedly be there for them.

When we draw our dying breath in this earthly life, we will not be judged by how many projects we completed, how far up the ladder we managed to climb, or how many careers we succeeded at; rather we will be judged only and explicitly by how much we loved.

St. John of the Cross said, "At the end of our life we shall be judged by love." And according to Blessed Teresa of Calcutta, "Sanctity consists of nothing else but a firm resolve." We all possess the ability to firmly resolve to become a saint and please our Lord with lives of love. No one else chooses our destiny for us. The choice for holiness is ours.

PRAYER IN HONOR OF ST. THÉRÈSE

Oh, dear St. Thérèse, Blessed Teresa chose to take your name because she loved you so. Please help me to see the sublimity in simplicity and help me to learn from your "little way." Please help me to strive to become reliant on God's holy will in my life. Help me to be like you so I may crave to do good in Heaven, not just here upon earth. Amen.

GUARDIAN ANGEL, GUIDE ME

Dear Guardian Angel, please remind me that you are a very real spirit, a servant of God, who is always beholding God's face in Heaven. You are truly here with me to protect and guide me all the days of my life. God has given you to me as a gift I should not squander. Tap me on the shoulder to remind me to strive to lead a virtuous life. Please stay nearby this day to guide and protect me with your watchful care as I strive to guide and protect my children. Amen.

EIGHT

Splinters from the Cross and the Kiss of Jesus

A living love hurts. Jesus, to prove his love for us, died on the Cross. The mother, to give life to her child, has to suffer. If you really love one another properly, there must be sacrifice. — Blessed Teresa of Calcutta

Humanity's future depends on people who rely on the truth and whose lives are enlightened by lofty moral principles that enable their hearts to love to the point of sacrifice. — Pope John Paul II

Intertwined with the unending joys and rewards of motherhood are the sacrifices, sorrows, and suffering that a mother endures. From childbirth on, a mother's love encompasses many of life's challenging situations and the attendant worry, anguish, or heartache. A mother's time and energy are sacrificed as she lovingly raises her children.

According to Blessed Teresa of Calcutta, "If you really love one another properly, there must be sacrifice." Why? Why must we sacrifice? And why must we suffer? We naturally desire happiness, which is really of divine origin. Humanly, we don't want to think about suffering or pain. We may even feel tempted to skip this chapter and get to the "happier" stuff!

Nonetheless, we learn from the *Catechism of the Catholic Church* (number 2015) that "The way of perfection passes by way of the Cross. There is no holiness without renunciation and spiritual battle. Spiritual progress entails the ascesis and mortification that gradually lead to living in the peace and joy of the Beatitudes."

> Blessed are the poor in spirit, for theirs is the
> kingdom of heaven.
> Blessed are the meek, for they shall inherit
> the earth.
> Blessed are those who mourn, for they shall be
> comforted.
> Blessed are those who hunger and thirst for
> righteousness, for they shall be satisfied.

Blessed are the merciful, for they shall
obtain mercy.

Blessed are the pure in heart, for they shall
see God.

Blessed are the peacemakers, for they shall be
called sons of God.

Blessed are those who are persecuted for righ-
teousness' sake, for theirs is the kingdom of
heaven.

Blessed are you when men revile you and
persecute you and utter all kinds of evil
against you falsely on my account. Rejoice
and be glad, for your reward is great in
heaven.

When we consider and really meditate on the Beatitudes, we begin to understand that true happiness,
peace, and contentment are not necessarily found in
this earthly life, in what the world considers to be happiness. Such rewards are not truly found in power,
riches, or human achievement; rather, true happiness,
peace, and contentment are found in being united with
God's love and living in union with him.

We learn from St. John of the Cross, "Would that
men might come at last to see that it is quite impossible

to reach the thicket of the riches and wisdom of God except by first entering the thicket of much suffering, in such a way that the soul finds there its consolation and desire. The soul that longs for divine wisdom chooses first, and in truth, to enter the thicket of the Cross."

Suffering and pain are assured realities of our life on earth. We cannot run or hide from them. As mothers, we are sometimes asked by God to suffer quietly for him. Little sacrifices, heartaches, or pain patiently carried can become redemptive. When offered up to God, these sufferings ultimately will be used as a means to our salvation and our family's salvation.

Greater sufferings will come as well; we don't have to search for them, but they never visit us without our having the sufficient grace to sustain us. While dealing with life's external challenges, we can retreat inward, soliciting the strength and grace that we possess deep in our souls, and we can supplicate our dear Lord for even more grace to endure our trials with love and patience. In so doing, we can help to initiate major changes in the hearts of our offspring. Truly, we can.

Another great saint, no stranger to suffering, St. Teresa of Ávila, said, "Observe that we gain more in a single day by trials which come to us from God and our neighbor than we would in ten years by penances and other exercises which we take up of ourselves." Amazing!

My spiritual director and friend, Father Bill, and I call these trials "God-made penances." We've often talked about how it is so much easier to take on our own penances, skipping a meal to fast or saying extra prayers, for instance, than to bear patiently and lovingly the wrongs committed against us or inconvenient sickness and pain, lovingly offering it all up to our Lord. But that is exactly where we will earn the most graces for ourselves and our families. We don't have to go out and look for these penances and opportunities for grace. They will come to us! Our Lord, the divine physician, knows exactly what we need and when we need it!

✎ *Paradoxical Promises*

As we draw closer to Christ and begin to really live the Beatitudes, we come closer to achieving lasting and genuine peace and happiness living in union with our Lord. This peace cannot be shaken; it is divine. No one can rob us of this peace of soul.

The Beatitudes are the paradoxical promises that sustain our hope in the midst of suffering and sacrifice. They pronounce the rewards that are already waiting for us. We need to read through the Beatitudes and really meditate on them, not just skim through the words. They invite us to empty our hearts, purify them, and seek God's love above everything. We begin to realize that God alone can satisfy our craving for happiness, and we pray that we can someday embrace the Cross.

John Paul II expressed to us in his apostolic letter *Novo Millennio Ineunte* that the faithful are called to experience "the paradoxical blending of bliss and pain" when following our Lord. It is never all bliss or all pain. But throughout the pain and suffering, there will be joy of heart, a divine joy that will transcend our beings and will convert others.

Sometimes a mother may suffer because she feels unappreciated by her family members or those around her who don't think highly of a mother's role. Sometimes this is due to the mentality of our society that suggests that we are only as valuable as our paycheck. Especially at these times, we must recall Jesus' great love for mothers. He transcended the norms of his own culture and treated women with great dignity, respect, and tenderness. We need to heed the great leaders of our Church, such as Pope John Paul the Great and Benedict XVI, who have always promoted women culturally, socially, and politically while still defending our gift of motherhood.

When we experience challenging times as mothers, we draw strength from the promises of the Beatitudes. Even the Blessed Mother was not exempt from suffering. She partook in her son Jesus' suffering.

We can recall Blessed Teresa's words saying that if we "really love one another properly there must be sacrifice." All of the graces we need to carry on will be provided just for the asking. Let's not forget to ask.

We can seek union with God by an act of our will. This is not a passing or temporary affection of the heart.

∾ *Embracing the Cross*

When Blessed Teresa forever preached, "Keep the joy of Jesus ever living in your heart, and keep smiling," many people generally assumed that this living saint was always in a privileged state of spiritual ecstasy, in union with God. What did she have to suffer about?

Everyone loved her and accepted her. She must always have felt loved and comforted by God as well. In reality, like so many of us, she quietly struggled with feelings of loneliness and abandonment by God during a long dark night of the soul that our Lord gifted her with.

Nevertheless, she continued to serve the poor every day with a smile, spreading joy to all around her. That visible radiance of love and joy taught others to smile and spread joy as well. Her smile wasn't a mask to hide her pain and suffering, but a real manifestation of her deeper genuine joy. Blessed Teresa also professed, "Joy is a net to catch souls." She lived what she preached.

Blessed Teresa's willingness and ability to embrace the Cross and continue to smile gives us hope as mothers. We are consoled knowing that throughout the difficult moments of our vocations when we may not feel our Lord's love or presence, he is present and will never abandon us.

St. Thérèse of Lisieux, the "Little Flower," whom Blessed Teresa loved, said, "Do not believe I am swimming in consolation; oh, no, my consolation is to have none on earth." St. Thérèse was happy when she did not feel consolation because she knew God must be truly working in her life.

While we may or may not be expected to embrace the Cross as tightly as Blessed Teresa of Calcutta, St. Thérèse of Lisieux, or any of the other great saints, we should know that we, too, are called to patience and loving endurance in the suffering that comes to us, whatever it may be. Whether we suffer little annoyances or great tragedies, God's grace will sustain us. When we accept our penances and sufferings with prayer and trust, God's love will radiate a light in us leading the way for others.

Thank God for the gift of faith that sustains our hope no matter what. Even when all of our plans or good intentions seem to fall apart or do not proceed in the manner in which we had hoped, we hang onto God's promises for us; we remain faithful in his service, and he will perform the miracles in human hearts.

Our Holy Father Pope Benedict XVI told us in his first encyclical, *Deus Caritas Est,* "Faith, hope, and charity go together. Hope is practiced through the virtue of patience, which continues to do good even in the face of apparent failure, and through the virtue of humility, which accepts God's mystery and trusts him even at times of darkness, Faith tells us that God has given his Son for our sakes and gives us the victorious certainty that it is really true: God is love!"

At a time when I was going through a tremendous trial, Blessed Teresa of Calcutta told me, "If we pray, it will be easy for us to accept suffering. In all our lives suffering has to come. Suffering is the sharing in the passion of Christ. Suffering is the kiss of Jesus, a sign that you have come so close to Jesus on the Cross that he can kiss you." Hmmm, Jesus can kiss me. Jesus is kissing me? What an incredible, humbling, and overwhelming thought.

I'll never forget another time when Mother Teresa told me she had tried to console a little girl who was suffering with a painful illness, using a similar analogy about Jesus' kiss for her. Blessed Teresa said the little girl responded by whispering, "Jesus, that's enough kisses, please stop kissing me." Oh, the honesty and innocence of a child!

St. Thérèse taught us how to truly give ourselves over totally to God when she said, "I understood that to become a saint, one must suffer much, one must always choose the most perfect path and forget oneself; I understood that each soul is free to respond to the calls of our Lord, to do little or much for him, in a word, to select among the sacrifices he asks. Then I cried out, 'My God, I choose everything.' I will not be a saint by halves. I am not afraid of suffering for Thee."

There is no escaping the Cross and the life of the Beatitudes. Eventually, by God's grace, we will not look to run from the Cross; rather, we will be certain that by living the life of the Beatitudes, we will indeed become holy, bring others hope, and will deeply please our Lord.

"Often the deepest cause of suffering is the very absence of God," Pope Benedict XVI told us in *Deus Caritas Est*. We must have faith that God is present, even when he appears to be silent or absent from us. He is merely purifying our souls of passions and hindrances and preparing them for the unimaginable blessedness of divine union. And if we really listen we may hear him whisper to our hearts.

ST. FRANCIS, GUIDE ME

Dear St. Francis, you loved Jesus to the point of accepting the sacred stigmata. You embraced the spirit of poverty and preached peace with extreme passion. Help me to also be an instrument of Christ's peace, sowing love, pardoning injuries, promoting faith, hope, and love, and spreading joy. Ask our Lord to grant me the graces I need to fathom his promises to those who live the life he asks of us and to know without a doubt that it is in dying to ourselves, living a life of grace and clinging to our Lord, that we will be assured of eternal life. Amen.

ST. MICHAEL, PROTECT US

Dear St. Michael the Archangel, so powerful over all evil, defender of the just, please assist me as I raise my children. Please steer my family clear from all evil and harm of body and of soul. Amen.

NINE

Everyday Miracles

The best and surest way to learn the love of Jesus is through the family. Whatever you do in your family for your children, for your husband, for your wife — you do for Jesus. — Blessed Teresa of Calcutta

Each morning we open our eyes to a brand-new day full of hope, promise, challenge, and opportunities. "How will we use this day?" we ask ourselves.

Even our best-laid plans and intentions may not see their way to fruition. The care of our family and household can mean that all of the items on what we thought should be our "to do list" just might not get checked off. Attempting to keep up with the never-ending care of our family — including housework, mounds of laundry, and a kitchen sink that seems to automatically refill with dirty dishes — can cause us to feel tired, disappointed, or inadequate.

On the days when we do not see the fruits of our work — errands completed, phone calls made, clean laundry nicely folded, kitchen counters sparkling, and floors dust-free — we need to reevaluate what is most important in life.

When we are feeling particularly unaccomplished, it's wise to reflect for a few moments on the events that have, in fact, filled our days. We need to remember those smiles that we brought to our children's faces, after drying their tears and cheering them up. How about all the sibling squabbles we refereed? What about our role of peacekeeper and treaty maker?

Then there was that walk out in the fresh air that we took with our young ones. It was not only healthy and a welcome change, but educational as well, since we talked about nature and about God, who fills the earth with beauty.

Maybe that trip to the grocery store with the crew provided us with more than just the essentials for this week's meals. Perhaps it also served as an opportunity for a short discussion about what foods are healthy and body-building and which ones are junk foods. (I say "short discussion" because there is not a whole lot of time for in-depth articulation as we try to put the sugar-coated, pink- and purple-dyed snacks back on the shelves and quickly zoom down the aisle before the kids grab some more attention-grabbing stuff!)

We guide our children through the course of their day, reminding them to do their homework, pick up after themselves, take their showers and baths, and then reward their good behavior with lots of praise. We can teach them about cleanliness and responsibility when we recruit them to help with household chores.

Bringing them together in prayer around the dinner table, keeping them focused on what's really important, and encouraging them to think of others are not easy tasks in today's world. Yet these lessons are invaluable in helping to build our children's characters and mold their consciences.

Let's start every day with prayer. Each time we open our eyes to a new day, we have a wonderful opportunity to start with a new resolve to serve God even more lovingly. It is a practice that takes only a few minutes but can help transform an insignificant day into something quite beautiful and even holy.

We should offer our hearts to God every morning, giving him our day fully without reserve. We must ask him what he wants of us. He knows our heart. In his divine providence he has put us in the heart of our home to do his will, to shepherd his flock and feed his sheep in our domestic church.

Sometimes we kneel down by ourselves in the early morning, stealing away a few moments before the busyness starts in, our head bowed, yearning for quiet time with the Lord, and in bursts a child, crying from a nightmare or up earlier than ever, starving for breakfast. That is God, in control. No need to fret about lost time with our Lord. He is there, and we serve him in our children.

We must also remind ourselves that our love for our Lord is not a mere feeling, it is our desire and our decision to love him. We won't always feel or be aware of his presence. But we continue to reach up in faith, offering up our hearts every morning and really every minute of our lives.

Throughout our busy days there are many opportunities to lift our hearts to God, asking for grace and guidance. We just need to want it, and we can indeed find moments to seek divine grace and to give thanks for his many blessings. Pope John Paul II told us, "God comes to us in the things we know best and can verify most easily, the things of our everyday life." He surely must have been thinking of mothers!

Many miracles are worked in human hearts by our lives of love, prayer, and dedication to the sanctification of our family members. We may not always be aware of them, but we should trust that we are God's instrument in our families and in the world.

St. Edith Stein said, "Woman's soul is fashioned to be a shelter in which other souls may unfold. Both spiritual companionship and spiritual motherliness are not limited to the physical spouse and mother relationships, but they extend to all people with whom woman comes into contact." That's why our Lord made women's hearts so soft and tender!

The intrinsic sacredness of motherhood is a mystery and miracle almost unfathomable. Our hearts can understand this sublimity, though, and that is just where we feel our sense of accomplishment.

Blessed Teresa told me, "Christ calls us to be one with him in love through unconditional surrender to his plan for us. Let us allow Jesus to use us without consulting us by taking what he gives and giving what he takes." And this we mothers try to do each day.

Talk about everyday miracles. One morning years ago, I realized what a powerful word "church" is and how God can use a single word to work a miracle, when I was at the bus stop with my children. My three-year-old daughter, Mary-Catherine, stood with me as we said good-bye to her older brother Joseph and sister Jessica.

That particular morning, Mary-Catherine had insisted on wearing one of her church dresses to the bus stop. Because we were in a rush as usual to make the bus, I didn't object to her fashion choice too much.

Within minutes, the bus arrived and quickly took off again, taking our children to school. My neighbor and I stayed behind at the bus stop to chat for a bit. She admired Mary-Catherine's dress and told my daughter that she looked very beautiful.

"It's really her church dress, but she really wanted to wear it today," I told her.

To my surprise, my neighbor's eyes welled up with tears, and she began pouring her heart out to me about her father's last wishes on his deathbed.

I was surprised to see her suddenly appear sad and begin a serious discussion, seemingly out of the blue. Where did this come from?

My neighbor managed to get a few words out. "My father made me promise when he was in the hospital dying that I would have my son baptized," she told me.

"I never did," she said, and then she couldn't hold back the tears and began to sob.

I tried to reassure her that it was not too late. Since her son was eight years old, she was embarrassed and afraid that the priests would criticize her for waiting so long. So with each passing year, she struggled with her conscience, feeling that the situation was hopeless.

We ended up talking for quite some time at the bus stop that morning, while my daughter twirled around in her fancy red dress. I told my neighbor that I would be happy to make a call ahead to the rectory if she would like me to set up a meeting for her to go in and speak with one of our priests. After she thought about it, she began to calm down and seemed more peaceful, hoping that it would turn out all right.

We parted with a big hug. I brought Mary-Catherine home to have her breakfast and I called our parish priest. Father told me that he would be looking forward to meeting with this woman. I relayed the message to my neighbor, who went ahead and set up the appointment.

My neighbor went to confession after a very long absence from Church and the sacraments. She arranged her son's baptism and felt a tremendous weight lifted from her heart. They began to attend church regularly.

After that, she seemed to smile much more readily. Her demeanor was much calmer and more peaceful.

Her son joined our religious education program. My neighbor began to volunteer in the religious education office while her son was at his weekly class. She enjoyed helping and felt she was giving back. She met other moms who helped out as well, which gave her a feeling of belonging.

Who would think that a persistent little girl in a fancy red dress would play a part in helping to bring about a mother's return to the Church and her son's baptism, bringing him into the Church, as well?

Who would think that the mention of the word "church" at the right time in the right place would actually work a miracle? It is amazing when we are allowed to get a glimpse of God's work, of actually seeing that miracles really happen on ordinary days in the midst of our ordinary lives. That is why it is of great magnitude for us to ask God to use us to fulfill his holy will. We absolutely need to offer our days to him to use us as he wills.

Thank God for pretty little girls in their pretty little dresses! Every day is another chance and opportunity to draw closer to our Lord and to bring others to him.

◆ ◆ ◆

Let us go forward in peace,
our eyes upon Heaven,
the only one goal
of our labors.

> — St. Thérèse
> of the Child Jesus

PRAYER IN HONOR OF
POPE JOHN PAUL THE GREAT

Oh, dear John Paul the Great, tireless loving shepherd, you taught us by your example to strive to become close to the Blessed Virgin Mary, the surest means of becoming closer to her Son, our Lord and Savior Jesus Christ. Pray for us so that we may always persevere in our search for Jesus in our lives. You inspired the world by your life of total dedication and surrender to the will of our Lord and guided us while you were intimately united with the Blessed Mother. We know that as you lived your life under Mary's mantle, you called upon her always to guide your steps as you emulated the words "To Jesus through Mary." You lived and died with your motto, "Totus Tuus," meaning "I am totally yours." When you could no longer speak, due to the progression of your illness, you then wrote the words "Totus Tuus."

Please help me and all mothers to "be not afraid" as you have preached on so many occasions, the first time being on the steps of St. Peter's. Pray that we will have confidence in our role as the heart of the home raising our children and helping them to work out their salvation so that we may not just make it to Heaven one day, but also bring with us many souls who have been inspired to turn to Jesus because of our loving example. Totus Tuus! Amen.

PRAYER TO JESUS AND MARY: HELP ME TO BE FAITHFUL TO PRAYER

Dear Lord Jesus, help me to be faithful to prayer. Help me to know without a doubt the great value and significance of an ongoing conversation with you. Help me to seek out moments here and there throughout my busy days to offer my heart to you. Teach me to also strive to make more time to be with you in prayer. Help me to remember and always be mindful that, as Blessed Teresa said, what I do to others, I do to you. Allow me to see that many graces are attached to the work in the home through my life of prayer, sacrifice, and service, as my family works out its salvation. Thank you for giving a mother the great reward of Heaven!

Remind me, please, that you silently work many miracles in human hearts even at the times I cannot see anything, so I may be patient and loving as my family grows in holiness. Keep me steadfast in my faith and prayer, knowing that as I am the heart of my home, my family relies on my faith, love, prayers, and example. Allow my faith to grow as I draw ever closer to your most Sacred Heart, my Lord. I love you! I trust in you!

As we look to the example of the Holy Family for inspiration, please, dear Mother Mary, help my family turn to prayer often and grow in holiness together in the beautiful and profound blessing that is our family. Help us learn from you so Blessed Teresa's prayer may be answered and someday our home will become as another Nazareth. Amen.

TEN

A Conversation with the Divine

Therefore, I tell you, all that you ask in prayer, believe that you will receive it, and it shall be yours.

— Mark 11:24

It should never be forgotten that prayer constitutes an essential part of Christian life, understood in its fullness and centrality. Indeed, prayer is an important part of our very humanity: it is the first expression of man's inner truth, the first condition for authentic freedom of spirit.

— Pope John Paul II, *Familiaris Consortio*

Prayer is a conversation with the Divine. We draw closer to God each time we visit with him, during visits to the Blessed Sacrament, at Mass, in dealings with our family, and in the recesses of our hearts where he dwells. We can visit and converse with God at any time. He tells us, "I thirst." He thirsts for our love.

Although we know that a mother prays throughout her daily tasks of loving service within her family, there will also be times when a mother can find the luxury of time, a quiet place and another posture for prayer. A mother's prayer is very efficacious and pleasing to our Lord no matter where and when she prays. But when she is able to put aside a special time for prayer in which to meet Jesus, she may choose a place and a posture where her prayer pleases herself fully as well.

A quiet place, as free from distraction as possible, is important. We should take time to settle down and feel relaxed, wherever we may be. Concentrating on one's breathing can help us find inner quiet, setting aside thoughts that clutter our mind.

Now we can become aware of the presence of God. We can pronounce the name of Jesus over and over again deep in our heart, not with our lips. This will bring us into the awareness of God's abiding presence.

Blessed Teresa instructs those who pray and want to come closer to God to "hunger for his presence." As we hunger for him, we should tell him just that. We love him and desire him and want to come closer. We want to know his love for us. We want to do his will.

As we rest in God's presence, we wait for his personal message, for us and we respond to him in gratitude and love as we are moved by the Holy Spirit.

When we are more accustomed to coming before the Lord, seeking him entirely, we will learn to unite ourselves with him no matter where we are or what we are doing. The noise and bustling around us won't matter. The pulls on our attention won't matter. Our conversation with him will pervade each moment of our lives because it will be with each breath.

We must all find the time for prayer, never giving up on prayer. And we should teach our children the value of prayer. God is always waiting. He longs to draw us even nearer to him still.

Dear Lord, thank you for this incredible gift of motherhood! Please accept the gift of my heart kneeling before you as I mother my children.

Sources

Benedict XVI, Pope. *Deus Caritas Est*, encyclical, 2006.

———. General audience, April 2006.

Catechism of the Catholic Church, with modifications from Editio Typica, 1994.

John Paul II, Pope. *Christifidelis Laici* (On the Vocation and the Mission of the Lay Faithful in the Church and in the World), post-synodal apostolic exhortation, 1988.

———. *Evangelium Vita* (The Gospel of Life), encyclical, 1995.

———. *Familiaris Consortio* (The Role of the Christian Family in the Modern World), apostolic exhortation, 1981.

———. *Mulieris Dignitatem* (On the Dignity and Vocation of Women), apostolic letter, 1988.

———. *Novo Millennio Ineunte* (At the Beginning of the Third Millennium), apostolic letter, 2001.

Louis de Montfort, St. *True Devotion to Mary*, 1941.

———. *The Secret of the Rosary*, 1954.

Thomas Aquinas, St. *Summa Theologica*, 1947.

Vatican Council II. Decree on the Apostolate of the Laity (*Apostolicam Actuositatem*), 1965.

———. Dogmatic Constitution on the Church (*Lumen Gentium*), 1964.

Acknowledgments

For all of the mothers in my life:

To my mother, Alexandra Mary Uzwiak Cooper, in loving memory and gratitude for bringing me into this world against doctor's orders and raising me with her tender love and grace in our large family. She taught me the necessity of prayer and how to give without ever counting the cost.

In loving memory and gratitude to my grandmother Alexandra Theresa Karasiewicz Uzwiak, for her inexhaustible love, guidance, and inspiration. Her smile, her laugh, and her lessons of love and prayer live on in my life.

To my godmother, Aunt Bertha Uzwiak Barosky, in gratitude for her loving prayers and guidance throughout my life which she continues in her sweet optimistic way to bestow upon me even now.

In loving memory of Blessed Teresa of Calcutta, in gratitude for her cherished lessons of love and holy living that have deeply inspired me. Her consistent encouragement to me to continue to write to help others has certainly given me much courage and motivation. I thank her for her poignant and tender words at the beginning of this book and her quotes throughout. Her faith in me and love for me has left a permanent imprint on my heart.

To dear Mother Mary, our Blessed Mother, who has always watched over me during my entire lifetime, in gratitude for her motherly influence, love, and protection that has forever been my saving grace.

To all others I hold dear:

In loving memory of my father, Eugene Joseph Cooper, who along with my mother brought me into this world, in gratitude for his love and support and his working hard to care for our large family.

To my brothers and sisters — Alice Jean, Gene, Gary, Barbara, Tim, Michael, and David. Thank you for all the great times throughout the years. Thank you for loving me.

To my very dear friend and spiritual guide, Father Bill C. Smith: thank you for your cherished friendship, love, and guidance. Your amazing guidance has certainly helped to mold me into who I am. I will forever be thankful.

To my husband, David, my partner and best friend: my heart still skips a beat when you come near. Thank you for believing in me and loving me. You continue to be the wind beneath my wings.

In loving memory of an amazing and saintly person of our time: dear Pope John Paul the Great, in gratitude for his inexhaustible wisdom and blessings in the profound and selfless love of his shepherding, which I was able to benefit from throughout a good part of my lifetime.

Additionally, I thank you, dear Lord Jesus, for putting me still and on complete bed rest during my precarious pregnancy, inspiring and enabling me to write down my thoughts, prayers, and reflections on pregnancy and motherhood so these words may be shared with other mothers along the pilgrimage of motherhood. Thank you, dear Lord, for your love!

I would also like to thank Gwendolin Herder, Roy M. Carlisle, and John Jones at Crossroad Publishing for having faith in me to go forward with this book. It was very providential to meet Roy and John on that Feast of the Immaculate Heart of Mary and being given the opportunity and privilege to talk with them about my work. I thank them for being a very important part of this book's coming to fruition.

About the Author

Donna-Marie Cooper O'Boyle speaks to a mother's heart about the blessings, grace, and lessons learned throughout her spiritual journey during motherhood. She has received awards for her work and is the author of the best-selling book *Catholic Prayer Book for Mothers* (OSV, 2005), which was endorsed by Blessed Teresa of Calcutta and given the prestigious honor of an apostolic blessing from Pope John Paul II.

Donna-Marie grew up in a large, close-knit Catholic family, admiring God's majesty in the beauty of nature surrounding her as she sought out holiness and searched for a deeper meaning in life.

Embracing family life, she became a mother of five. She also served as a Prioress and Mistress of Novices for the Third Order of St. Dominic, founded a branch of the Lay Missionaries of Charity, taught religious education as a catechist for over twenty years, and was a Eucharistic minister to the sick. She founded the Angels of Mercy, the Marian Mothers, Apostles of the Blessed Sacrament, and Friends of Veronica, an outreach to senior citizens. She is a lay Missionary of Charity.

In God's divine providence, Donna-Marie crossed paths with Blessed Teresa of Calcutta and remained in contact with her for a decade. Donna-Marie is passionate about sharing her inspiration and "heart-to-hearts" she had with her beloved friend Blessed Teresa of Calcutta with other mothers, to encourage them and help them to see the sublimity in their vocation. Donna-Marie lectures on topics relating to Catholic women and can be reached at her Web site, *www.donnacooperoboyle.com*.

A Word from the Editor

There was something about her sincerity that intrigued me. And there was also something about her earnestness that piqued my interest in what she was writing. Donna and I and John, my editorial colleague from Crossroad, were sitting at a table with 20,000 publishers, booksellers, agents, authors, media people, and international publishing friends milling around the floor of the Jacob Javits Convention Center in New York. This was the BookExpo, which is the annual convention of the whole "trade" publishing industry in the United States (the word "trade" in this sense refers to the non-textbook, non-scholarly normal book publishing world of fiction and nonfiction), all gathered to celebrate the coming publication of new books that would be arriving in bookstores that fall. It is never easy to have a conversation in hubbub like that, but on this warm June day the three of us were making the attempt. As Donna is a winsome and persuasive speaker, we soldiered on in the midst of the cacophony.

Donna had a new book of prayers for Catholic mothers that was about to be published. That was encouraging to me because it is so hard to get published these days. My natural thought was that if another house was taking the risk on her work then maybe she was worth our taking that risk. (This is how most publishers think.) And it is difficult to get published, although the numbers of new books each year would seem to belie that fact. When I started my career in publishing back in the late 1970s, about 50,000 new books a year were issued. In the last few years that number has risen to a high of 172,000. What is deceptive about that number is that the majority of those books are published by small and online publishers rather than by larger and/or New York–based houses that have recognizable names (like Crossroad). Unfortunately, the explosion of Internet Web sites and e-mail has turned thousands of typists into would-be "writers," many of whom would not be publishable within what most professionals define as "normal parameters." But they are publishing in droves, and today you can find book after book, if you are even a tiny bit Internet savvy, that you would never have found bound between two covers two decades ago. And yet, despite the plethora of new books coming off the "presses" each year, it is difficult for bona fide writers to publish their work. My early assessment was that Donna had the real goods and was clearly someone who was determined to navigate her way through the labyrinth of the established publishing world. She was not going to settle for just setting up a blog to share her prayers with a few friends.

As an aside, years ago I had a conversation with Richard Tam, who started *iUniverse.com,* the best known of the Internet/print-on-demand start-ups in this new slice of our industry. *iUniverse.com* was so hyped in press releases and publishing circles that the large Barnes & Noble bookstore chain even had taken a large financial stake in the company. Richard said that he believed that editors like me were doomed to extinction within five years and that all of regular book publishing would disappear with me. His thesis was that the authors and writers should be the ones who decide what is published into the book marketplace, and editors like me should not have the power of the "gatekeeper" to say whose book does or doesn't get published. That conversation was about seven years ago. His naiveté about how the book as a physical object and as a result of cultural dynamics actually functions in a mass culture like America's surprised me. He admitted that he knew next to nothing about our industry. Although he was wrong in innumerable ways, he accurately predicted that many people would use the Internet to self-publish and that this would alter the world of publishing markedly.

Donna was making her case, and I probably listened more intently and paid more attention to what she wanted to do with her next writing projects than I might have with someone who had never been published. It is hard to admit that, but it is true. Which is why I have consciously focused on finding new authors who have great ideas for books but who have never been published. In fact, my instinct for doing this is not seen normally as what a senior-level editor could or should be doing. But I relish the accomplishment of launching new writers on their publishing careers, and it is one thing that feels most creative about my work.

So once we finally settled on motherhood as the subject of her next book, we began the normal collaborative process. Again Donna surprised me. I thought this might be challenging for her because our editorial process is, well, thorough — a nice way to describe it. And her first book of prayers did not require this kind of intensive editorial work. But she rose to the challenge and even acted as if she enjoyed it. (She was probably cursing me in her dreams, but she was very patient and kind.)

Now I saw a whole other side of Donna. Obviously she was determined and persuasive, but now I saw her commitment to growth as a writer in her responses to every tiny stylistic or grammatical change, to every query for clarification or expansion or deletion of text, i.e., to every suggestion that the copyeditor and I made for revising the text. I even had her go back and put together a bibliography, which at one point was not thought to be necessary for the book. She didn't blink or complain.

Her passion and humility are combined in such a way that she really can navigate life based on faith in a Presence greater than herself. It is that combination that must have been recognized by Mother Teresa and Pope John Paul II. Once you meet her in this book you will see what I have seen: that God shows up in these unusual ways, in ordinary but extraordinary people. I count it a privilege to have worked with Donna on this book. I hope you enjoy it as much as I have enjoyed working with her.

Roy M. Carlisle
Senior Editor

Of Related Interest

H. J. Fischer, Veteran Vatican Journalist
POPE BENEDICT XVI
A Personal Portrait

The All-New, Definitive Biography of
POPE BENEDICT XVI

Inspired by the author's
thirty-year personal and professional relationship
with Joseph Ratzinger.

H. J. Fischer is the ideal biographer of the new
Pope. As a theologically trained journalist, a friend
of Joseph Ratzinger, and a twenty-five-year Vatican
correspondent for Germany's leading daily newspaper,
Dr. Fischer has observed and accompanied the profes-
sor and cardinal for three decades. He understands the
life and work of this gifted church leader as well as the
challenges and questions that confront Benedict XVI
in his new role.

Includes more than sixty color and black-and-white photos.

0-8245-2372-5, $19.95, hardcover

crossroad

Of Related Interest

Carole Hallundbaek
DEAR LITTLE ONE
Thoughts to My Child in an Uncertain World

Assembled as a precious gift book, these profound and loving reflections of hope and wisdom draw us into the special intimacy of the parent-child relationship. Reflections include: New Life, You Are Never Alone, Marriage, Humility, and many others.

0-8245-2312-1, $14.95, hardcover

Check your local bookstore for availability.
To order directly from the publisher,
please call 1-800-707-0670 for Customer Service
or visit our Web site at *www.cpcbooks.com.*
For catalog orders, please send your request to the address below.

THE CROSSROAD PUBLISHING COMPANY
16 Penn Plaza, Suite 1550
New York, NY 10001

All prices subject to change.

crossroad